A HISTORICAL GUIDE TO

Walt Whitman

HISTORICAL GUIDES
TO AMERICAN AUTHORS

The Historical Guides to American authors is an interdisciplinary, historically sensitive series that combines close attention to the United States' most widely read and studied authors with a strong sense of time, place, and history. Placing each writer in the context of the vibrant relationship between literature and society, volumes in this series contain historical essays written on subjects of contemporary social, political, and cultural relevance. Each volume also includes a capsule biography and illustrated chronology detailing important cultural events as they coincided with the author's life and works, while photographs and illustrations dating from the period capture the flavor of the author's time and social milieu. Equally accessible to students of literature and of life, the volumes offer a complete and rounded picture of each author in his or her America.

A Historical Guide to Ernest Hemingway
Edited by Linda Wagner-Martin

A Historical Guide to Walt Whitman
Edited by David S. Reynolds

A Historical Guide to Ralph Waldo Emerson
Edited by Joel Myerson

A
Historical Guide
to Walt Whitman

EDITED BY
DAVID S. REYNOLDS

New York   Oxford
Oxford University Press
2000

A historical guide to Walt
Whitman

Oxford University Press

Oxford   New York

Athens   Auckland   Bangkok   Bogotá   Buenos Aires   Calcutta
Cape Town   Chennai   Dar es Salaam   Delhi   Florence   Hong Kong   Istanbul
Karachi   Kuala Lumpur   Madrid   Melbourne   Mexico City   Mumbai
Nairobi   Paris   São Paulo   Singapore   Taipei   Tokyo   Toronto   Warsaw

and associated companies in
Berlin   Ibadan

Library of Congress Cataloging-in-Publication Data
A historical guide to Walt Whitman / edited by David S. Reynolds.
p.   cm. — (Historical guides to American authors)
Includes bibliographical references and index.
ISBN 0-19-512081-7; ISBN 0-19-512082-5 (pbk.)
1. Whitman, Walt, 1819–1892—Criticism and interpretation.
2. Literature and history—United States—History—19th century.
I. Reynolds, David S., 1948– .   II. Series.
PS3238.H57   1999
811'.3—dc21   99-12608

1 3 5 7 9 8 6 4 2

Printed in the United States of America
on acid-free paper

Contents

Abbreviations

BDE   Thomas L Brasher. *Whitman as Editor of the Brooklyn Daily Eagle.* Detroit: Wayne State University Press, 1970.

CH   *Walt Whitman, the Critical Heritage.* Ed. Milton Hindus. New York: Barnes & Noble, 1971.

DN   Whitman. *Daybooks and Notebooks.* Ed. William H. White. 3 vols. New York: New York University Press, 1978.

GF   *The Gathering of the Forces.* Ed. Cleveland Rodgers and John Black. 2 vols. New York: G. P. Putnam's Sons, 1920.

ISit   Whitman. *I Sit and Look Out: Editorials from the Brooklyn Daily Times.* Ed. Emory Holloway and Vernolian Schwartz. New York: AMS Press, 1966.

LGC   Whitman. *Leaves of Grass, Comprehensive Reader's Edition.* Ed. Harold Blodgett and Sculley Bradley. New York: New York University Press, 1965.

NUPM   Whitman. *Notebooks and Unpublished Prose Manuscripts.* Ed. Edward F. Grier. 6 vols. New York: New York University Press, 1984.

NYA   *Walt Whitman of the New York Aurora.* Ed. Joseph J. Rubin and Charles H. Brown. State College, Penn.: Bald Eagle Press, 1950.

NYD   Whitman. *New York Dissected.* Ed. Emory Holloway and Ralph Adimari. New York: Rufus Rockwell Wilson, 1936.

PW   Whitman. *Prose Works, 1892.* Ed. Floyd Stovall. 2 vols. New

York: New York University Press. *Vol. I: Specimen Days* (1963); *Vol. II: Collect and Other Prose* (1964).

TC   Whitman. *The Correspondence.* Ed. Edwin Haviland Miller. 5 vols. New York: New York University Press. *Vol. I: 1842–67* (1961); *Vol. II: 1868–75* (1964); *Vol. III: 1876–85* (1964); *Vol. IV: 1886–89* (1969); *Vol. V: 1890–92* (1969).

UPP   *The Uncollected Poetry and Prose of Walt Whitman.* Ed. Emory Holloway. 2 vols. Gloucester, Mass.: Peter Smith, 1972.

WCP   Whitman. *Complete Poetry and Collected Prose.* Ed. Justin Kaplan. New York: Library of America, 1982.

WEP   Whitman. *The Early Poems and the Fiction.* Ed. Thomas L. Brasher. New York: New York University Press, 1963.

WWC   Horace Traubel. *With Walt Whitman in Camden.* 7 vols. Vol. I (1905; rpt., New York: Rowman and Littlefield, 1961); Vol. II (1907; rpt., New York: Rowman and Littlefield, 1961); Vol. III (1912; rpt., New York: Rowman and Littlefield, 1961); Vol. IV (1953; rpt., Carbondale: Southern Illinois University Press, 1959); Vol. V (Carbondale: Southern Illinois University Press, 1964); Vol. VI (Carbondale: Southern Illinois University Press, 1982); Vol. VII (Carbondale: Southern Illinois University Press, 1992); Vol. VIII (Oregon House, Cal.: W. L. Bentley, 1996); Vol. IX (Oregon House, Cal.: W. L. Bentley, 1996).

A HISTORICAL GUIDE TO
Walt Whitman

Introduction

David S. Reynolds

One of America's most beloved and influential writers, Walt Whitman (1819–1892) brought a radical democratic inclusiveness to literature, transforming the diverse, sometimes pedestrian images of his culture into soaring, fresh poetry through his exuberant personality. He opened the way for modern writers by experimenting with innovative social and sexual themes and by replacing rhyme and meter with a free-flowing, prose-like poetic form that followed the natural rhythms of voice and feeling.

Few books of poetry have had so controversial a history as Whitman's brash, erotically charged *Leaves of Grass*. When the volume's first edition appeared in 1855, some prudish reviewers branded it as obscene and egotistical. "A mass of stupid filth" was the verdict of the fastidious critic Rufus Griswold.[1] The Boston *Intelligencer* similarly labeled it "a mass of bombast, egotism, vulgarity, and nonsense."[2] Even the discerning Henry David Thoreau, while generally enthusiastic about Whitman, wrote of *Leaves of Grass*, "It is as if the beasts spoke."[3]

In the face of such attacks, Whitman took pains to minimize explicit sexual images in later poems he wrote for his ever-expanding volume, six editions of which were published in his lifetime. His increasing attention to themes of religion, patriotism, and technological progress, coupled with his selfless service as a volunteer nurse in the Civil War hospitals, resulted in his being widely venerated as America's "Good Gray Poet." Still, attacks continued to come from some quarters. In 1882, Boston publisher James R. Osgood was forced to stop printing the book's sixth edition when the city's district attorney, Oliver Stevens, ruled that *Leaves of Grass* violated "the Public Statutes concerning obscene literature"; this episode gave rise to the phrase "banned in Boston."[4]

It was Whitman's frankness about heterosexual eroticism that most raised eyebrows in the nineteenth century. That was the era when in polite circles the repression of sex could be taken to absurd extremes: piano legs were frequently covered in frilly stockings, undergarments were called "inexpressibles," and nude sculptures in museums were sometimes decorously draped in gauze. It is small wonder that some readers were shocked by a poet who, in his opening poem, announced his urge to go "undisguised and naked" in the woods, who described a lonely woman yearning to caress twenty-eight young men swimming nude in a nearby stream, and who evoked sexual intercourse, as in the lines "Thruster holding me tight and that I hold tight! / We hurt each other as the bridegroom and the bride hurt each other."[5]

Most nineteenth-century reviewers did not take special note of what today seem to be the homosexual undercurrents of *Leaves of Grass*. Because Whitman's treatment of male comradeship was in keeping with then-current mores of same-sex love (the term "homosexuality" was not used in English until 1892, the year the poet died), his "Calamus" poems, which to many modern readers seem clearly homoerotic, elicited far fewer outcries than his poems of heterosexual intimacy, especially "A Woman Waits for Me" and "To a Common Prostitute." During the Boston banning, the latter two poems were named as particularly offensive. Amazingly, even the tame poem "A Dalliance of the Eagles," about the mating of a male bird and a female bird in midair, came under the Boston ban, as did some twenty-two scattered references to heterosexual passion in other poems. The fact that the innocent "Dalliance" was targeted while all but one of the forty-five "Calamus" poems were allowed to stand tells much about the era's moral tastes, which were ridiculously squeamish about heterosexual love but still permissive of same-sex affection, which was not generally associated with sexual passion. Similarly, two Whitman anthologies of the period, Ernest Rhys's *Leaves of Grass: The Poems of Walt Whitman* (1886) and Arthur Stedman's 1892 collection of Whitman's *Selected Poems*, omitted many of the heteroerotic images while retaining the homoerotic ones, which were deemed conventional enough to be included in these scrubbed, polite volumes designed for the Victorian parlor.

The issue of the contemporary response to Whitman's sexual images points up a larger topic that is the basis of the current volume: Whitman cannot be adequately understood unless he is placed fully in his unique historical moment. To be sure, his poetry, like all great literature, transcends its era and speaks eloquently to later generations. But the fact that it still moves us does not mean that we can recklessly impose today's ideas or values on it. However enlightened our ideas on topics like sex, class, or race may be, we are doing a disservice to Whitman if we ignore his own cultural contexts and bend his writings to fit our own priorities. "In estimating my volumes," he wrote, "the world's current times, and deeds, and their spirit, must first be profoundly estimated."[6] The poet fails, he wrote, "if he does not flood himself with the immediate age as with vast oceanic tides [. . .] if he be not himself the age transfigured."[7]

Whitman's writings were indeed "the age transfigured," reflecting virtually all aspects of nineteenth-century life. His poetry emerged in the 1850s, when the nation was on the verge of unraveling due to the quarrel over slavery that led to the Civil War. Whitman, a former political hack who had edited Brooklyn's leading Democratic newspaper and had written conventional poetry and fiction, was startled out of his complacency by the specter of impending disunion. No longer a party loyalist, he had come to believe that the nation was threatened on all sides by corruption and moral flabbiness. Of President Franklin Pierce, the soft-spined chief executive who leaned to the South, Whitman wrote, "The President eats dirt and excrement for his daily meals, likes it, and tries to force it on The States."[8] Horrified by escalating tensions between the North and the South in the wake of the infamous Fugitive Slave Law of 1850 and the proslavery

Kansas-Nebraska Act of 1854, he wrote, "We need satisifiers, join-
ers, lovers. These heated, torn, distracted ages are to be com-
pacted and made whole."[9] The nation's merits and demerits, as
he called them, must be transformed in the crucible of poetry.

Describing the poet's all-unifying role, he announced, "One
part does not counteract another part, he is the joiner, he sees how
they join."[10] For Whitman, the times demanded a poet who could
survey the entire cultural landscape and give expression to the full
range of voices and images America had to offer.

Among these cultural voices were strident ones of anger and
protest. For a decade before the first edition of *Leaves of Grass* appeared, reformers of various stripes had been agitating for radical social change. Antislavery minister Henry Ward Beecher declared in 1851, "Agitation? What have we got to work with but
agitation? Agitation is *the* thing in these days for any good."[11]
Abolitionist lecturer Wendell Phillips asserted, "Republics exist
only on the tenure of being constantly agitated," a sentiment
echoed by his colleague Joshua Giddings, who said, "Agitation is
the great and mighty instrument for carrying forward re-
forms."[12] And Whitman's favorite politician, Free-Soil senator
John P. Hale, told Congress, "I glory in the name of agitator. I
wish the country could be agitated more vastly than it is."

Whitman thought that he, above all, was the one chosen to
agitate the country. He declared, "I think agitation is the most
important factor of all—the most deeply important. To stir, to
question, to suspect, to examine, to denounce!"[13] In the 1855
preface to *Leaves of Grass*, he announced that the poet is best
equipped to "make every word he speaks draw blood . . . he
never stagnates."[14] Key lines in his poems echo this zestful tone:
"I am he who walks the states with a barb'd tongue, questioning
every one I meet"; and "Let others praise eminent men and hold
up peace, I hold up agitation and conflict."[15] He never gave up
the spirit of agitation he shared with antebellum reformers. "As
circulation is to the air, so is agitation and a plentiful degree of
speculative license to political and moral sanity," he wrote in his
1871 prose essay *Democratic Vistas*. "*Viva*, the attack—the peren-
nial assault!"[16]

Agitation for Whitman did not mean joining a radical reform

group intent on revolutionizing the social order. To the contrary, he viewed reformers as potentially dangerous disrupters of society. During the slavery crisis, he berated both abolitionists and proslavery southern fire-eaters, both of whom were calling for the immediate separation of the North and the South. As a newspaper editor in the 1840s, he fumed, "Despising and condemning the dangerous and fanatical intensity of 'Abolitionism'—as impracticable as it is wild—the *Brooklyn Eagle* as much condemns the other extreme from that."[17] Although he believed in the social and political advancement of women, he took no part in the many women's rights conventions that succeeded the historic one in Seneca Falls, New York, in 1848. Likewise, even though his liberated attitude toward sex had much in common with that of the free-love advocates of his day, he had little tolerance for the free-love movement. Although he featured working-class types in his poetry, he did not accept working-class radical movements such as Fourierist socialism or, later on, communism and anarchism. When his left-leaning aficionado Horace Traubel hounded him on his political stance, he advised, "Be radical, be radical, be radical—be not too damned radical."[18]

While advocating agitation, therefore, Whitman took care to avoid excessive radicalism. For example, Whitman, a devotee of the Union, could not identify with abolitionist William Lloyd Garrison, who, in disgust over slavery, burned the Constitution in public and thundered, "Accursed be the AMERICAN UNION, as a stupendous republican imposture!"[19] Nor could he, an ardent advocate of the marriage institution, go along with the free-lovers, who wanted to abolish conventional marriage because they regarded it as legalized prostitution. For all his adventurousness, he had a definite conservative streak, an impulse to avoid extremes and steer a political middle course. It was perhaps for this reason that he shied away from homosexual activists, especially British writer John Addington Symonds, who pressed him to make a clear declaration of his homosexuality. In the early 1870s, Symonds began barraging Whitman with questions on the matter; Whitman later recalled that these questions aroused in him a "violently reactionary" response "strong and brutal for no, no, no."[20] When, in 1890, Symonds asked point-blank whether the

"Calamus" poems portrayed what was then called "sexual inver-
sion," Whitman angrily insisted that such "morbid inferences"
were "damnable" and "disavow'd by me."[21]

It could be, as some have claimed, that Whitman was telling
the truth when he denied being an active homosexual. Informa-
tion about the poet's sex life is slim: there is strong evidence that
he had at least two fleeting affairs with women around the time
of the Civil War, and he had a number of passionate (whether or
not physical) relationships with young men. Most likely, though,
his denial to Symonds was emblematic of his lifelong impulse to
defuse any controversial topic that could prove deleterious to his
personal or social peace. He witnessed enough disruption among
his family members—his father's financial struggles, the pathetic
retardation of his brother Eddy, the psychotic episodes of his sister Hannah, the confirmed insanity of his brother Jesse, whom
Walt had to commit to the Brooklyn Lunatic Asylum—to make
him want, at all costs, to avoid further disorder in his private life.
That's why, when he was in the throes of his stormy relationship
with Washington streetcar conductor Peter Doyle, he warned
himself to "depress . . . this diseased, feverish, disproportion-
ate adhesiveness" and cultivate "a superb calm character."[22]
Hence also his idealized self-portrait in the 1855 preface; as he described himself "the equable man" who could handle all things
"grotesque or eccentric."[23]

It is significant that this poetic balancing act began in 1847, the
year President James Polk intensified the war against Mexico in
an effort to take over hundreds of millions of acres of land in
what is now the American West. For antislavery northerners like
Whitman, the Mexican War was part of an infamous plot by the
South to capture new land where slavery might be planted. This
specter of the westward expansion of slavery induced Henry
David Thoreau to refuse to pay his local poll tax, leading to the
one-night incarceration in the Concord jail immortalized in his
protest essay "Civil Disobedience." Whitman, a Free-Soiler who
had editorially opposed slavery extension in the *Eagle*, was prepared neither to go to jail for his beliefs nor to demand immediate disunion, as the Garrisonians were doing. Instead, his first instinct was to write poetry in which the two sides of the slavery

divide were held in friendly equilibrium. In his notebook, he scribbled the first known lines of the kind of free-flowing, prose-like verse that would become his stylistic signature.

I am the poet of slaves and of the masters of slaves,[. . .]
I go with the slaves of the earth equally with the masters
And I will stand between the masters and the slaves,
Entering into both so that both shall understand me alike.[24]

Whitman here invents a poetic "I" who can comfortably mediate between the political antagonists whose opposing claims threaten to divide the nation. He announces himself simultaneously as the poet of "slaves" and of "the masters of slaves," one who is prepared to "go with" both "equally." He is able to "stand between" and "enter into" both. Emerging directly out of the slavery crisis, Whitman's poetic persona was constructed as an absorptive device that could imaginatively defuse rancorous sectional quarrels, just as in his private life Whitman cultivated a "superb calm character" to meliorate personal upheavals.

During the early 1850s, his alarm over rising national tensions intensified, and the absorptive, equalizing power of his "I" grew exponentially. For him, the poet was no marginal artist distanced from the social events of the day but rather a vital social agent necessary for national healing and reconciliation. He once referred to his "main life work" as the *"great construction of the new Bible."*[25] Indeed, he had messianic visions of changing the world through inspired poetry whose pulsating rhythms, as scholars have shown, owed much to the King James version of the Bible. "This is what you shall do," he instructed in the 1855 preface, ". . . read these leaves in the open air every season of every year of your life."[26] Of all nations, he emphasized, the United States "most need poets." Since political leaders were failing miserably to hold the nation together, poets alone held the key to social cohesion. "The Presidents," he announced, "shall not be their common referee so much as their poets shall." The poet, he explained, "is the arbiter of the diverse and he is the key. He is the equalizer of his age and land . . . he supplies what wants supplying and checks what wants checking."

What he supplied in *Leaves of Grass* was a profoundly democratic vision in which all barriers—sectional, racial, religious,
spatial, and sexual—were challenged in unprecedented ways.
Theoretically, American democracy had itself abolished social
barriers. By the 1850s, however, it had become painfully clear that
such barriers were on the verge of separating the nation. Whitman's poetic persona affirmed complete equality. At a time when
the North and the South were virtually at each other's throats,
Whitman's "I" proclaimed himself, "A southerner soon as a
northerner, / . . . At home on the hills of Vermont or in the
woods of Maine or the Texan ranch."[27] In an era when racial
conflict was exacerbated by the slavery debate and by surging im-
migration, he painted sympathetic portraits of Native Americans, recently arrived Europeans, and African Americans—even
to the extent of identifying himself with a fugitive slave: "I am
the hounded slave . . . I wince at the bite of dogs, / Hell and
despair are upon me." During a period when class divisions were
prompting American socialists to establish scores of classless
communities throughout the country, he forged a poetic utopia
in which the rich and the poor, the powerful and the marginal co-
existed in diversified harmony. This thoroughly democratic "I"
was, in the words of "Song of Myself":

Of every hue and trade and rank, of every caste and religion,
Not merely of the New World but of Africa Europe or Asia . . .
    a wandering savage,
A farmer, mechanic, or artist . . . a gentleman, sailor, lover or
    quaker,
A prisoner, fancy-man, rowdy, lawyer physician or priest.

Whitman hoped that America would learn from his example
of total democracy. He ended the 1855 preface by announcing
confidently, "The proof of the poet is that his country absorbs
him as affectionately as he has absorbed it."[28] Such absorption,
however, was long in coming. True, perceptive readers such as
Emerson, Swinburne, and Rossetti recognized the wondrous
power of Whitman's verse. "I greet you at the beginning of a
great career," Emerson wrote him in a letter, saying his poetry

"has the best merits, namely of fortifying and encouraging."[29] But *Leaves of Grass*, which had attempted to abolish all narrowness of vision, immediately became subject to narrow interpretations. A number of critics fixed on its sexual images, giving rise to a long debate between those who branded Whitman as obscene and those who insisted that he treated sex candidly and purely. Leading the defense was the fiery reformer William Douglas O'Connor, who brilliantly nicknamed Whitman the "Good Gray Poet," a sobriquet that did much to defuse opponents and emphasize the poet's benign, avuncular qualities.

But the "Good Gray" image itself proved confining, as Whitman increasingly turned away from daringly experimental themes and toward more conventional ones. The Civil War, he thought, accomplished for the nation what he had hoped his poetry would by blowing away many social ills and bringing to power Abraham Lincoln, the homespun "captain" who possessed many of the egalitarian qualities Whitman had assigned to his poetic "I." In Lincoln's life—and especially in his tragic death—America was rescued, Whitman thought, because at last it had a martyred authority figure it could worship without shame. Whitman devoted much of the last three decades of his life to eulogizing Lincoln and the war, repeatedly giving his lecture "The Death of Abraham Lincoln" and reading "O Captain! My Captain" before reverent audiences.

Confused by the complex social realities of Reconstruction, Whitman retreated to a moderately conservative stance on issues such as race and class. Radical activists—free-lovers, feminists, communists, religious iconoclasts—continued to flock to him, using progressive passages from his early poems to promote their individual causes. But he maintained a genial distance from their programs, insisting that his work could be understood only in its relation to the totality of American culture.

It has not been much easier for modern readers to see the whole Whitman than it was for his contemporaries. Just after his death, his friends and followers—later dismissed as the "hot little prophets"—deified him in hagiographic books and articles. Then came the Freudian revisionists, from Jean Catel through Edwin Haviland Miller and David Cavitch, who portrayed him as a deeply conflicted man driven by neuroses ranging from father hatred to repressed homosexuality. Individual schools of critics have, predictably, claimed Whitman as their own. For the New Critics, Whitman is the master of language experimentation. For deconstructionists, he is the ever-elusive poet whose meanings inevitably sink into an abyss of indeterminacy. For feminists, his occasionally conservative statements about women have counted less than his ringing endorsements of the equality of the sexes. For queer theorists, almost everything in his verse can be traced to his sexual orientation.

How would Whitman have viewed the various interpretations? Individually, he probably would have said, each is narrow and reductive; taken together, they begin to approach the wholeness of his poetry. "No one can know *Leaves of Grass*," he declared, "who judges it piecemeal."[30] The problem with most critics, he stressed, was that they "do not take the trouble to examine what they started out to criticize—to judge a man from his own standpoint, to even find out what that standpoint is."

The current volume attempts to judge Whitman from his own standpoint by evaluating his life and work in the context of his times. My capsule biography demonstrates the close affinity between the poet's life and major currents in society and culture. Ed Folsom's essay demonstrates that Whitman's treatment of race reflected larger cultural phenomena, from the insurrectionary spirit of the 1850s to the complex circumstances of Reconstruction. Jerome Loving traces Whitman's ambivalent views on social class—sometimes radical, sometimes conservative—to opposing attitudes on the topic that circulated in antebellum America. M. Jimmie Killingsworth probes the homosexuality issue, evaluating some of Whitman's most confessional poems against the background of a society in which clear notions of sexual types had not yet evolved. Roberta K. Tarbell reveals the profound influences of art and artists on the poet's sensibility, and Kenneth Cmiel links *Leaves of Grass* to the theory and practice of American democracy.

By exploring a wide spectrum of historical dimensions in Whitman, this volume attempts to capture the spirit of the poet who declared, "I am large, I contain multitudes." Whitman would surely endorse an effort to ground his poetry in a society whose invigorating diversity was the chief source of his all-encompassing vision.

NOTES

1. *CH*, 32.
2. *CH*, 61.
3. *The Correspondence of Henry David Thoreau*, ed. Walter Harding and Carl Bode (Westport, Conn.: Greenwood, 1974) 444.
4. Oliver Stevens to James R. Osgood, letter of March 1, 1882. Feinberg Collection, Library of Congress.
5. *WCP*, 27, 47.
6. *WCP*, 23.
7. *WCP*, 1310.
8. *NUPM*, I:96.
9. *WCP*, 10.
10. *LGC*, 344.
11. In Paxton Hibben, *Henry Ward Beecher: An American Portrait* (1927; rpt., New York: Press of the Readers Club, 1942), 187.
12. Phillips, *Speeches, Lectures, and Essays* (1884; rpt., New York: Negro University Press, 1968), 53; Giddings, quoted in Eric Foner, *Free Soil, Free Labor, Free Men: The Ideology of the Republican Party before the Civil War* (New York: Oxford University Press, 1970), 112. The statement by Hale quoted in the next sentence is also on 112.
13. *WWC*, V:529.
14. *WCP*, 9.
15. *LGC*, 342, 237.
16. *PW*, II:383, 386.
17. *Brooklyn Daily Eagle*, December 5, 1846.
18. *WWC*, I:223.
19. *Selections from the Writings and Speeches of William Lloyd Garrison* (New York: Negro University Press, 1968), 119.
20. *WWC*, I:77.
21. *TC*, V:71.
22. *NUPM*, II:887, 886.
23. *WCP*, 8.

24. *NUPM*, I:69.

25. *NUPM*, I:353.

26. *WCP*, 11. The following quotations in this paragraph are on 8–9.

27. *WCP*, 42. The following quotations in this paragraph are on 65 and 43.

28. *WCP*, 26.

29. *LGC*, 729–30.

30. *WWC*, I:116. The next quotation in this paragraph is from *WWC*, IV:41.

Walt Whitman
1812–1892

A Brief Biography

David S. Reynolds

Walt Whitman emerged from a humble background to become one of America's most celebrated poets. The second of eight children of Walter and Louisa Van Velsor Whitman, he was born on May 31, 1819, in the rural Long Island village of West Hills, about fifty miles east of Manhattan. Although his ancestors were not distinguished, he later placed great emphasis on his genealogy. In his poem "By Blue Ontario's Shore," he wrote, "Underneath all, Nativity, / I swear I will stand by my own nativity."[1]

He made much of his dual ancestry—English on his father's side, Dutch on his mother's. He believed he got a "Hollandisk" firmness from his mother's ancestors and a certain obstinacy and willfulness from the "paternal English elements."[2] His paternal lineage reached back to Zechariah Whitman, who came to America from England in the 1660s and settled in Milford, Connecticut. Zechariah's son Joseph resettled across the sound in Huntington, Long Island, where he became a local official and a landholder. He acquired large tracts of land that became known as "Joseph Whitman's Great Hollow." His sons acquired even more land, and his grandson Nehemiah built what became the family homestead on a 500-acre farm in the West Hills area of Huntington. Nehemiah's wife, Phoebe (better known as Sarah), chewed tobacco, swore freely, and fired commands at the slaves who tilled the land.

The large Whitman landholdings were slowly dissipated over the generations. The poet's father retained a sixty-acre portion of the Whitman land. A carpenter and sometime farmer, Walter Whitman, Sr, built a two-story house there around 1810 and six years later moved into it with his wife. According to some sources, he was a moody, taciturn man whose temperament was at least partly captured in the famous lines "The father, strong, self-sufficient, manly, mean, anger'd, unjust, / The blow, the quick loud word, the tight bargain, the crafty lure."[3]

Still, biographers who claim that the poet was locked in oedipal conflict with his father overstate the hostility of their relationship. His brother George would say, "His relations with his father were always friendly, always good."[4] Most of Walt's recollections of his father were, in fact, affectionate. In old age, he told stories of his father's love for cattle and children. He recalled fondly the pride his father took in his house-building skills, which for the poet represented the bygone artisan work habits threatened by rising industrialism. Also, he inherited from his father freethinking and democratic sympathies.

His mother, Louisa Van Velsor Whitman, came from a Long Island Dutch family that had established a homestead in Woodbury, not far from the Whitman land. His maternal grandmother, Naomi (Amy), was a genial Quaker woman whose death in 1826 was one of the great sorrows of his youth. His grandfather, the florid, hearty Major Cornelius Van Velsor, raised horses that the young Walt sometimes rode on Saturdays. Often the major perched the boy beside him on his farm wagon as he made the long ride across poor roads to deliver produce in Brooklyn.

Walt's mother, though unlearned and sometimes querulous and hypochondriac, was a loving woman with a vivid imagination and a gift for storytelling. She faced difficult circumstances: her husband's uncertain moods, financial instability, and, apparently, some problematic children, two of whom (Jesse and Hannah) would develop emotional problems and one of whom (Edward) was retarded and possibly epileptic from birth. Still, four of her children—George, Mary, Jeff, and Walt himself—approached normalcy. A good housekeeper and family peacemaker, she was often portrayed idealistically by the poet: "The mother at home quietly placing dishes on the supper-table, / The mother with mild words, clean her cap and gown, a wholesome odor falling off her person as she walks by.[5]

In May 1823, Walter Whitman took his pregnant wife and three young children from West Hills to seek his fortune in Brooklyn as a house carpenter. For a decade, he tried to take advantage of a real estate boom by building and selling small frame houses. Although he was a skilled carpenter, he did not have a good head for business, and he struggled financially. The Whitmans lived in no fewer than seven houses in Brooklyn in a decade. Of these houses, Walt would write, "We occupied them, one after the other, but they were mortgaged, and we lost them."[6]

A village of around 7,000 when the Whitmans moved there, Brooklyn was entering a period of rapid growth that by 1855, would make it the fourth-largest city in the nation. Walt Whitman spent twenty-eight years of his life there and often spoke of its influence on him. "I was bred in Brooklyn," he said later, "through many, many years, tasted its familiar life."[7] Located between rapidly urbanizing Manhattan to the west and rural Long Island to the east, Brooklyn for Whitman was a middle ground between the two, with access to both. In the 1820s, it still had characteristics of a country town. Its dusty, unpaved streets turned easily into mud after storms. Pigs and chickens roamed the streets, feasting on the garbage that was thrown there because of the lack of organized waste disposal. Still, Brooklyn was well situated on the East River, with ferry crossing to Manhattan, and its economy was expanding rapidly. As Whitman later commented, "Indeed, it is doubtful there is a city with a better situation in the world for beauty, or for utilitarian purposes."[8]

Among the many public celebrations and festivals held there during his youth, he especially recalled the one held on July 4, 1825, for the Marquis de Lafayette, the revolutionary war hero, who was making a tour of America. Lafayette rode in a coach to the corner of Cranberry and Henry streets, where he laid the cornerstone for the Apprentice's Library. In later retellings of the event, Walt claimed that the hero lifted several of the village children in his arms, among them the six-year-old Walt, whom he kissed on the cheek.

There was just one public school in Brooklyn, District School No. 1 on Concord and Adams streets. Walt attended it from 1825 (possibly earlier) until 1830. Run according to the old-fashioned Lancastrian system, which emphasized rote learning and rigid discipline, the school offered primary students a basic curriculum that included arithmetic, writing, and geography. Walt's teacher, B. B. Hallock, would recall him as "a big, good-natured lad, clumsy and slovenly in appearance." Apparently, Walt was a mediocre student, since Hallock, after learning later he had become a famous writer, said, "We need never be discouraged over anyone."[9]

Walt's education was supplemented by his early exposure to two liberating philosophies: deism and Quakerism. His father, a Jeffersonian rationalist who had known Thomas Paine in his youth, subscribed to the *Free Enquirer*, the radical journal edited by Frances Wright and Robert Dale Owen. Wright, widely denounced by conservatives as "the Red Harlot of Infidelity" because of her feminist and freethinking views, elicited Walt's lifelong admiration. Her deistic novel, *Ten Days in Athens*, was one of his childhood favorites. His background in deism doubtless shaped his famous proclamation that his was the greatest of faiths and the least of faiths—the greatest in his belief in God and everyday miracles, the least in his acceptance of any particular church or creed.

Another important influence on him was the Quaker faith, specifically the views of the Quaker leader, Elias Hicks. When Walt was ten, his parents took him to hear the eighty-one-year-old Hicks preach at Morison's Hotel in Brooklyn. Hicks placed great emphasis on the inner light, which Quakers believe put humans directly in touch with God. This doctrine resonated within the poet, who would place total reliance on the inspired voice of the self, irrespective of scriptures and doctrines.

At eleven, Walt left school, apparently to help support his financially struggling family, and began a remarkably varied job career. He first worked as an office boy for two Brooklyn lawyers,

James B. Clarke and his son Edward. The elder Clarke got him a subscription to a circulating library. Walt avidly read *The Arabian Nights*, Walter Scott's novels, and other adventurous works. By the summer of 1831, he was apprenticed to Samuel E. Clements, the editor of the Democratic weekly *Long Island Patriot*. After Clements was fired due to a scandalous lawsuit, Walt continued his training under the *Patriot's* foreman printer, William Hartshorne, a cheerfully sedate, elderly man who had personal reminiscences of George Washington and Thomas Jefferson.

In the summer of 1832, a terrible time of cholera, Walt's parents moved back to the West Hills area of Long Island. Walt stayed in Brooklyn, working as a compositor for the *Long-Island Star*, a Whig weekly run by the vibrant Alden Spooner. Walt remained with Spooner nearly three years, after which he worked for a compositor in Manhattan. These early printing jobs exposed him to the artisan work arrangements that were threatened by changing print technology. Walt had to do much of the typesetting for these publications by hand, a painstaking but, for him, rewarding activity that presaged his instinct to govern the printing of his poetry with a strong, controlling hand. "I like to supervise the production of my books," he would say, adding that an author "might be the maker even of the body of his book (—set the type, print the book on a press, put a cover on it, all with his own hands)."[10]

In 1836, after a huge fire destroyed many buildings in Manhattan's printing district, Whitman returned to Long Island and began a six-year stint as a roving schoolteacher. His first two teaching posts were in the villages of Norwich and West Babylon, where his family lived successively in 1836. During this time, he stayed with his family, which consisted of his parents and seven siblings: his older brother, Jesse, who may already have gone to sea; his sisters, Mary and Hannah; Edward, the youngest; and three other brothers with patriotic names—George Washington, Thomas Jefferson, and Andrew Jackson. In an autobiographical story written a few years later, "My Boys and Girls," Whitman wrote, "Though a bachelor I have several boys and girls I call my own." He described Hannah sentimentally as "the fairest and most delicate of human blossoms," Jeff as "a fat, hearty, rosy-cheeked youngster," and Mary as a beautiful but vain girl with "misty revealings of thought and wish, that are not well." Playfully, he told of carrying the "immortal Washington" on his shoulders, teaching "the sagacious Jefferson" how to spell, and tumbling with Andrew Jackson.[11]

In the spring of 1837, Whitman moved to other villages throughout Long Island, teaching a basic curriculum in tiny one-room schoolhouses. His salary was meager—in Smithtown, for instance, he got a paltry $72.50 for five months of teaching—but he economized by boarding with the families of students. In the spring of 1838, he temporarily abandoned teaching and founded a weekly newspaper in Huntington called the *Long-Islander.* Not only did he serve as the paper's editor, compositor, and press-man, but also each week he did home delivery by riding his horse, Nina, on a thirty-mile circuit in the Huntington area.

Evidently averse to entrepreneurship, he sold the paper after ten months and unsuccessfully sought another printing job in Manhattan, after which he worked in the Long Island town of Jamaica as a typesetter for the *Long Island Democrat,* edited by Democratic partisan James J. Brenton. For the *Democrat,* Whit-man wrote a series of articles titled "The Sun-Down Papers." Among these essays was a moralistic one that denounced the use of tobacco, tea, and coffee and another that allegorically repre-sented the uncertainty of religious truth. After a year of working for the *Democrat,* he returned to teaching, though he stayed on for a while as a boarder with the Brentons. Mrs. Brenton, dis-turbed by his habit of lounging under an apple tree and dream-ing the day away, found him lazy, uncouth, and not fit to associ-ate with her daughters.

As a teacher, he received mixed reports. One of his students in Little Bayside, Charles A. Roe, later recalled him as a beardless, ruddy-faced young man who dressed in a black coat with a vest and black pants.[12] His free, easy attitude toward his students was reflected in a mild approach to teaching that was similar to the progressive theories of education reformers such as Horace Mann and Bronson Alcott. Instead of drilling his students and punishing them harshly, as under the old Lancastrian system, he told amusing stories and drew them out by asking provocative questions. While such relaxed teaching methods impressed Roe, they had little appeal for Whitman's successor at a school in Woodbury, who sneeringly remarked that "the pupils had not gained a 'whit' of learning" under Whitman.[13]

By 1840, country teaching had become wearisome for Whitman. In a series of recently discovered letters to a friend, Abraham Leech, he branded the residents of Woodbury as "contemptible ninnies," who dragged him on long huckleberry outings and fed him greasy ham, boiled beans, and moldy cheese. Dubbing Woodbury "Devil's Den" and "Purgatory Fields," he wrote with exasperation, "O damnation, damnation! Thy other name is school-teaching and thy residence Woodbury." Calling himself "a miserable kind of dog," he complained that he was spending the best part of his life "here in this nest of bears, this forsaken of all Go[d]'s creation; among clowns and country bumpkins[,] flat-heads, and coarse brown-faced girls, dirty, ill-favored brats, with squalling throats, and crude manners, and bog-trotters, with all the disgusting conceit, of ignorance and vulgarity."[14]

Although he would later famously sing praise to the worth of ordinary people, at this point they struck him as ill-bred and re-pulsive. Whitman's snobbish attitude in the Woodbury letters corresponds with his appearance in the earliest surviving da-guerreotype of him, which shows a dandyish young man in a dark frock coat, with a fashionable black hat, a heavily polished cane, and a look of slightly disdainful sophistication.

His activities immediately after leaving Woodbury in early September 1840 are unclear. He continued to write articles for Brenton's *Democrat* until November. There is a sensational story, first related by Katherine Molinoff and discussed in my book *Walt Whitman's America*, that, in the winter of 1840, he taught in the eastern Long Island village of Southold, where allegedly he was run out of town by a group of enraged citizens after being de-nounced from the pulpit for having performed sodomy with some of his male students.[15] Based on hearsay and circumstantial evi-dence, this story awaits solid documentation. Until real proof sur-faces, we are well advised to follow the lead of most Whitman biographers, who accept his recollection that during this period he was teaching at a school in Whitestone, a village just north of

Brooklyn. He once scribbled in his notebook: "Winter of 1840, went to white stone [*sic*], and was there till next spring."[16] In May 1841, he wrote his friend Leech that he would be remaining in Whitestone "for some time to come," but before the end of the month he had abandoned schoolteaching altogether and had plunged into the world of Manhattan journalism.[17]

From 1841 to 1845, Whitman worked as a printer in Manhattan, edited newspapers for short periods, and wrote derivative poems and stories for magazines such as the *Democratic Review*. His temperance novel, *Franklin Evans*, published in 1842 as a cheap pamphlet to promote the Washingtonian movement, was a didactic potboiler that sold some 20,000 copies. Although these early writings are individually undistinguished, they show him experimenting with a variety of themes and images that he would later transform in his major poetry. From 1846 to early 1848, he edited the *Brooklyn Daily Eagle*, a leading organ of the Democratic party. In his many editorials for the *Eagle*, he became embroiled in the political and social debates of the day. On the issue of slavery, he opposed the abolitionists, whom he found extreme, but was an early and ardent supporter of David Wilmot's proposal that slavery be excluded from any western territories acquired by the United States in its impending war with Mexico. In 1847, the slavery issue prompted him to write his first notebook jottings in what would later become his characteristic free-flowing style.

> I am the poet of slaves and of the masters of slaves,[. . .]
> I go with the slaves of the earth equally with the masters
> And I will stand between the masters and the slaves.[18]

His support of the Wilmot Proviso apparently alienated Isaac Van Anden, the conservative Democrat who owned the *Eagle*, for, by mid-January 1848, Whitman found himself without a job. Within three weeks, however, he was hired as a clipping and rewrite man for the *New Orleans Daily Crescent*. Accompanied by his fifteen-year-old brother, Jeff, he headed south and arrived on February 26 at New Orleans, a bustling city of 160,000 with an equally large floating population of visitors and sailors. As members of a staff of twelve, he and Jeff helped with office work and perhaps home delivery. Walt contributed a variety of articles to the *Crescent*, mainly lighthearted sketches of colorful people he saw about town. During his period in New Orleans, he evidently had a romantic relationship with a man, which he described in the original version of his poem "Once I Pass'd through a Populous City." He also noticed the beautiful octoroon women of New Orleans, "women with splendid bodies— . . . fascinating, magnetic, sexual, ignorant, illiterate: always more than pretty— 'pretty' is too weak a word to apply to them."[19] New Orleans seems to have deepened his sympathy for the South, which he would later eulogize: "O magnet-South! O glistening perfumed South! my South!"[20]

After three months, Walt had a falling-out with the owners of the *Crescent* over money matters. He and the homesick Jeff took a steamer north to St. Louis and Chicago, then east through the Great Lakes and down the Hudson to Brooklyn. Upon his return home, he again became embroiled in politics. Well known as an opponent to the westward spread of slavery, he was selected as one of fifteen delegates to represent Brooklyn at the convention in Buffalo of the newly formed Free-Soil party. The convention, which had all the excitement of a religious revival, was a two-day affair under the sweltering August sun. A crowd of 20,000 was kept at a fever pitch by forty-three speakers, who rallied them under the slogans "Free soil, free speech, free labor and free men!" and "No more slave states, no more slavery territory and no more compromises with slavery anywhere!"[21] A month after the convention, Whitman founded a newspaper, the *Brooklyn Freeman*. Supporting the Free-Soil presidential candidate, Martin Van Buren, he wrote, "Our doctrine is the doctrine laid down in the Buffalo convention." He warned readers against voting for anyone who would add to the Union "a single inch of *slave land*, whether in the form of state or territory."[22] Neither the *Freeman* nor the Free-Soil party, however, had a happy fate. Whitman's newspaper office was destroyed in a disastrous fire, and the Free-Soilers were roundly defeated in the presidential election in November.

Economic necessity forced Whitman in 1849 to open a small store in Brooklyn that sold miscellaneous items: pens, pencils, paper, musical instruments, and books. Soon the store was doubling as a print shop, and he ran it with Jeff until he sold it three years later. He continued to write for the local papers and late in 1849 briefly served as editor of a new penny paper, the *New York Daily News*, which suspended operation the following February.

Whitman was jarred back into political action by events on the national scene. Congress, trying to mend sectional differences over the slavery issue, passed compromise measures that included a stringent fugitive slave act, by which recaptured slaves would be denied jury trial and those who aided them would be fined or jailed. Like many other northerners, Whitman was outraged by the law. In "Dough-Face Song," he pilloried malleable northerners, such as Massachusetts senator Daniel Webster, who had betrayed their former antislavery principles by endorsing the act. He again attacked the law in "Blood-Money," comparing its supporters to Judas Iscariot, and in "The House of Friends," he impugned "Dough-faces, Crawlers, Lice of Humanity—[. . .] / Muck-worms, creeping flat to the ground, / A dollar dearer to them than Christ's blessing."[23] Swept up by insurrectionary fervor, he wrote another poem, "Resurgemus," in which he lamented the failure of the recent revolutions in Europe and predicted the eventual rise of the poor against their oppressors.

> Not a Grave of the slaughtered ones,
> But is growing its seeds of freedom,
> In its turn to bear seed
> Which the winds carry afar and resow.[24]

These political poems of the early 1850s are important transitional texts that prefigure *Leaves of Grass*. Once a loyal Democrat who wrote in straightforward journalese, Whitman was now writing powerfully rebellious poetry that for the first time in print used a form that approximated free verse. He would incorporate "Resurgemus" into *Leaves of Grass*, where it was retitled "Europe, the 72d and 73d Years of These States."

At this time, Whitman was living with his parents and siblings in Brooklyn in a house on Myrtle Street. From his print shop, he issued a short-lived guidebook, *The Salesman's and Traveller's Di-*

rectory for Long Island, and he wrote Long Island sketches for William Cullen Bryant's *Evening Post*. A familiar presence in the studios of local artists and sculptors, he was elected president of the Brooklyn Art Union. In March 1851, he gave an address to the group arguing the need for aesthetic appreciation in an increasingly materialistic age.

Trying to capitalize on the city's expansion, he adopted his father's trade of carpentry. Throughout the early 1850s, he bought small lots, built frame houses on them, and sold them. Initially, he had some success. By the spring of 1852, he had sold the Myrtle Street house and had built two houses on Cumberland Street. He moved into one of them with his family and rented out the other. But entrepreneurship was not the forte of one with a track record of contemplative indolence. His practical brother, George, later recalled, "There was a great boom in Brooklyn in the early fifties, and he had his chance then, but you know he made nothing of that chance."[25]

If he did not succeed financially, however, Whitman matured poetically. The early 1850s witnessed his transformation from a derivative, conventional writer into a marvelously innovative poet. The first edition of *Leaves of Grass*—the most revolutionary and inspired poetry volume produced in America to that time—appeared in the summer of 1855. The reasons for his poetic maturation, although impossible to pin down exactly, are nonetheless partly explainable if we explore the historical context.

The presidential election of 1852 had drawn him back into political action. Strongly opposed to both the aging Whig, Winfield Scott, and the pliable Democrat, Franklin Pierce, both of whom were weak on the slavery issue, Whitman in 1852 sent a letter of support to New Hampshire senator John P. Hale, the nominee of the antislavery Free Democratic party. Whitman wrote that he strongly hoped that under Hale "a real live Democratic party" would arise, "a renewed and vital party, fit to triumph over the effete and lethargic organization now so powerful and so unworthy."[26] When Hale went down to resounding defeat in November, Whitman's hopes for "a renewed and vital party" were dashed.

His faith in the political status quo sank even further with two disheartening events of 1854: the passage of the Kansas-Nebraska Act and the capture of fugitive slave Anthony Burns. One of the main harbingers of the Civil War, the Kansas-Nebraska Act overturned the Missouri Compromise by permitting settlers of the western territories to decide for themselves about slavery. Equally ominous, in Whitman's eyes, was the case of Anthony Burns, who had escaped from slavery early in 1854 but was recaptured in Boston, tried, ordered back to Virginia, and escorted in chains by federal troops to the ship that carried him back to captivity. The Burns case, infamous among abolitionists, inspired Whitman's bitter poem "A Boston Ballad," which, along with the earlier protest poem "Resurgemus," was one of two pre–1855 poems later integrated into *Leaves of Grass.*

In addition to the slavery issue, political corruption exasperated him. As historians have shown, the 1850s brought unprecedented corruption on all levels of state and national government.[27] In the 1855 preface to *Leaves of Grass,* he impugned the "swarms of cringers, suckers, doughfaces, planners of the sly involutions for their own preferment to city offices or state legislatures or the judiciary or congress or the presidency."[28] By the time he wrote his political tract "The Eighteenth Presidency!" (1856), he was comparing politicians to lice, maggots, venereal sores, and so forth. Though excessive and not wholly warranted, such outbursts reflected Whitman's desire to look outside the party system for hope and restoration.

Faced by what he considered the disunity and fragmentation of American society, he offered his poetry as a gesture of healing and togetherness. In the 1855 poems he brought together images and devices from every cultural arena. From Manhattan street life, he borrowed much from the real-life figure of the b'hoy (slang for boy). He famously described himself in a poem as "Turbulent, fleshy, sensual, eating, drinking, and breeding.[29] In reality, he was few of these things: he was no breeder, for he almost certainly had no children; he was only a convival drinker; and he was turbulent only on those rare occasions when his temper got the best of his generally calm demeanor. But the wild qualities he brags about in the poem were characteristic of the b'hoy, who was typically a butcher or other worker who spent af-

ternoons running to fires, going on target excursions, or prome-
nading on the Bowery with his g'hal. Whitman saw the b'hoy as
a wonderfully fresh American type. In his notebook he praised
"the splendid and rugged characters that are forming among
these states, or have already formed,—in the cities, the firemen
of Mannahatta, and the target excursionist, and Bowery Boy."[30]
One of his goals as a poet was to capture the vitality and defiance
of the b'hoy. His whole persona in *Leaves of Grass*—wicked
rather than conventionally virtuous, free, smart, prone to slang
and vigorous outbursts—reflects the b'hoy culture. One early reviewer noted that his poems reflected "the extravagance, coarse-
ness, and general 'loudness' of the Bowery boys," while another
generalized, "He is the 'Bowery Bhoy' in literature."[31]

While integrating the attitudes of common people, Whitman
also absorbed images from the kind of popular performances the
people loved. If his poetry has an unprecedented intimacy, as
though the poet were reaching right through the page to us, it
was partly because, as a cultural ventriloquist, he was poetically
enacting the kind of performances that he witnessed among
American actors and singers. During this time what was called
the American style of acting evolved. This style featured intense
emotionalism and, above all, a dissolving of the boundary between the performer and the audience. Few crossed this boundary so notably as Junius Brutus Booth, a leading tragedian whose
genius, Whitman said. "was to me one of the grandest revela-
tions of my life, a lesson of artistic expression."[32] So utter was
Booth's absorption in a role that he challenged the very bound-
aries between life and art. He could become so carried away as
Othello trying to suffocate Desdemona with a pillow that he had
to be pulled away by other actors for fear he would actually
kill her. He gave the kind of deeply felt performances that the
American public loved. Whitman himself was a kind of sponta-
neous actor, spouting Shakespeare passages on ferryboats or in
New York omnibuses. For him, acting provided not just a link to
the public but also a metaphor for flexible role-playing in his poetry. He pauses in a poem to boast of his role-playing ability: "I
do not ask the wounded person how he feels, I myself become
the wounded person."[33] In "Crossing Brooklyn Ferry" he says he

has "Play'd the part that still looks back on the actor or actress, / The same old role."

In music, his interest similarly gravitated to performers who had vital connections with the popular audience. The Hutchinsons, a family singing group that was the Beatles of the day, was the epitome of American singing for the poet who above all saw himself as the American singer. In a newspaper he wrote of the Hutchinsons, "Simple, fresh, and beautiful, we hope no spirit of imitation will ever induce them to graft any 'foreign airs' upon their 'native graces.' We want this sort of starting point from which to mould something new and true in American music."[34] His poetry in several ways imitated their singing. He loved what he called their "elegant simplicity in manner," and he told himself to maintain in his poems "a perfectly transparent, plate-glassy style, artless."[35] They sang about common American experience and ordinary individuals—as he said, "they are democrats"[36]— just he wished to be the bard of democracy. They were the first public figures to literally sing themselves. In their signature song, "The Old Granite State," well known to Whitman, they included all thirteen names of the members of their extended family. They made singing oneself a commonplace in the public arena. Whitman analogously wrote, "I sing myself," and brought his name into a poem: "Walt Whitman, an American, one of the roughs, a kosmos."[37]

His populist leanings controlled even his response to that relatively elite form of music, the Italian opera. "But for the opera I could not have written *Leaves of Grass*," he said.[38] The opera star he especially praised, the Italian contralto Marietta Alboni, was unique for him since she straddled the elite and the popular audience. She was not only a superb performer but also a musical bridge between the social classes. "All persons appreciated Alboni," he declared, "the common crowd as well as the connoisseurs; for her the New York theaters were packed full of New York young men, mechanics, 'roughs,' etc., entirely oblivious of all except Alboni."[39] He heard every one of her Manhattan concerts during her 1852 tour, and he tried to reproduce the feeling she inspired in several poetic lines: "I hear the trained soprano (what work with hers in this?) / She wrenches such ardors from me I did not know I possess'd them."[40]

His identification with his culture extended even to the most apparently private area—sex. Whitman has been normally viewed as a rebel against an absurdly proper Victorian America. True, there was an ice-cap of conventionality he was trying to pierce. But there was a seamy underside to his America. There was a thriving pornography trade that distressed him. He feared that such popular literature was contributing to what he regarded as America's alarming moral decline. Shortly after *Leaves of Grass* first appeared in 1855, he was walking around with a friend in Manhattan when he spotted a teenager selling pornographic books. "That's a New York reptile," he snarled. "There's poison around his fangs, I think."[41] He once wrote in his notebook: "In the pleantiful [*sic*] feast of romance presented to us, all the novels, all the poems really dish up only one . . . plot, namely, a sickly, scrofulous, crude, amorousness."[42] This love plot, Whitman believed, was at the very root of the problem of popular culture, for it was full of unhealthy distortions. In a newspaper article he wrote: "Who will underrate the influence of a loose popular literature in debauching the popular mind?"[43]

In opposition to this sensational popular literature, he wanted to treat sex as natural and genuine, free of hypocrisy and gamesmanship. To counteract what he saw as the corruptions and inhumanity of the love plot, Whitman borrowed sanitizing images from modern sciences, particularly physiology. The 1840s and 50s produced several books on human physiology that lent a new candor to the exploration of human sexuality. In the 1855 preface to *Leaves of Grass* he denounced literature "which distorts honest shapes" and wrote: "Exaggerations will be revenged in human physiology."[44] "Of physiology from top to toe I sing," he explained in one poem, describing his overall effort to deal with sex frankly and passionately, without the prurience of popular pornography.[45]

These and other cultural elements were fused in the crucible of Whitman's imagination. From genre painting and photography, he learned the value of crisp vignettes, which add color and sharpness to his long poetic catalogs. From optimistic forms of current philosophy, particularly Transcendentalism and Harmonialism, he absorbed an appreciation of self-reliance and symbolic perception.

This is not to say that *Leaves of Grass* is merely the sum of its historical parts. Something happened to Whitman privately that lay behind his poetic flowering. Did he have a mystical religious experience, as his early biographers insisted? Was he transformed by reading Emerson, as is suggested by his declaration to John Townsend Trowbridge that he had been simmering and Emerson brought him to a boil? Did he have a homosexual coming out, as some recent commentators have claimed?

Hard evidence in all of these areas is lacking. Suffice it to say that Whitman, by the mid-1850s, had become capable of writing all-encompassing poetry as a gesture of healing and togetherness to a nation he felt was on the verge of collapse. He had a messianic vision of his poems, as though by reading them America would be magically healed. "The proof of the poet," he wrote, "is that his country absorbs him as affectionately as he has absorbed it."[46]

Although his dream of being "absorbed" by his country was wildly overconfident, he did what he could to make it come true. He had been scribbling desultory snippets of poetry for years, using paper scraps and a notebook, but when he brought the passages together, added many new ones and a last-minute preface, he did so with a considerable amount of urgency. In the spring of 1855, he had 800 or so copies of his poems privately printed in Brooklyn. He filed for a copyright on May 15, and on July 5 the "first state" of the volume, with its wide and thin green binding and gold filigree lettering, was advertised for sale at local bookstores. In the course of the next six months, two more printings appeared, in slightly revised forms and at lower prices. In the hope of gaining attention and stimulating sales, Whitman not only had the book sent to distinguished Americans but also wrote three highly favorable reviews of the volume, which he planted in friendly newspapers.

The book immediately struck a chord among New England Transcendentalists. Ralph Waldo Emerson, the nation's leading philosopher, sent Whitman a glowing letter in which he praised the volume as "the most extraordinary piece of wit and wisdom that America has yet contributed. . . . I greet you at the beginning of a great career, which yet must have a long foreground somewhere, for such a start."[47] Two of Emerson's friends, Amos Bronson Alcott and Henry David Thoreau, were so impressed by *Leaves of Grass* that later they traveled to Brooklyn to meet its author.

The anonymously published reviews Whitman wrote of his own poetry show him pressing home his point that a totally American poet, free of European conventions, had arrived to announce new possibilities of cultural togetherness and cohesion. "An American bard at last!" he rhapsodized about himself in a piece for the *United States Review.* "He does not separate the learned from the unlearned, the northerner from the southerner, the white from the black, or the native from the immigrant just landed at the wharf."[48]

He may have seen himself as a unifier of his nation, but early reviewers did not agree. Although positive reviews of the first edition slightly outnumbered negative ones, some vigorously denounced its sexual explicitness and its egotistical tone. One reviewer blasted the volume as a "mass of filth," and another insisted that its author must be "some escaped lunatic, raving in pitiable delirium."[49]

Such harsh reactions may explain why Whitman changed tack when he came out with a second edition of *Leaves of Grass* the next year. The 1856 edition—a squat chunky volume in which every poem was titled and numbered—was in some ways quite different from the first edition, with its oversized binding and untitled poems. The new edition contained twenty new poems, making a total of thirty-two, as well as selected reviews and a public letter from Whitman to Emerson as backmatter. Despite these changes in packaging, Whitman's mission remained the same: to reach the American public with poetry that reflected both its tensions and its ideals. He professed confidence that widespread appreciation was forthcoming: "A few years, and the average annual call for my Poems is ten or twenty thousand copies—more, quite likely. Why should I compromise?"[50] But an underlying unease surfaced in a key change he made in his line about being accepted by his nation: "The proof of the poet shall be *sternly deferr'd* till his country absorbs him as affectionately as he had absorb'd it."[51] Deferral of widespread acceptance was to be even longer than he thought, for the 1856 edition met with meager sales and mixed reviews.

Now living with several members of his family in a modest frame house on Classon Avenue, Whitman looked like a rough satyr, broad-shouldered, and gray-bearded, wearing a striped calico jacket over a red flannel shirt and coarse overalls. When he was visited by Alcott and Thoreau, he seemed lazy and slow, enjoying stretching out on a couch for long talks. He told his visitors he loved to bathe outdoors well into the winter, ride the New York omnibuses, attend the opera, and, as he mispronounced it, "make pomes."[52] He gave a copy of his poems to Thoreau, who wrote in a letter to a friend that Whitman was "the most interesting fact at present," though he complained of the sexual frankness of the poetry.[53] For his part, Whitman admired Thoreau's self-reliance but lamented his "disdain—disdain for men (for Tom, Dick, and Harry): inability to appreciate the average life."[54]

Although he continued to write poems, Whitman also fantasized about reaching the people directly by becoming a traveling lecturer. In sketching plans to become a "wander-speaker," he announced his intention "to dart hither and thither, as some great emergency might demand," in an effort "to keep up living interest in public questions,—and *always to hold the ear of the people*."[55] He even printed a circular that advertised "Walt Whitman's Lectures," but nothing came of the project. Poetically, he was still driven by a messianic spirit. In June 1857, he identified "the principal object—the main life work" as the *"great construction of the new Bible*—the Three Hundred & Sixty Five."[56] Presumably, he aimed to produce 365 poems—a not unrealistic expectation, given that, at the time, he was writing so furiously that the third edition of *Leaves of Grass* would contain a hundred new ones.

In the meantime, he needed work, and he turned to his old vocation of newspaper editing. In the spring of 1857, he began contributing and perhaps for a time editing the *Brooklyn Daily*

Times, an established penny newspaper that he kept well stocked with sensational fiction, spicy news, and articles on all kinds of topics. His connection with the *Daily Times* lasted two years, until June 1859, when he left the paper apparently after a dispute with its owner over articles in which he recommended legalized prostitution and condoned premarital sex for women. In the summer of 1858, he had the first of many "sunstrokes," or dizzy spells, which would plague him for the next decade. He also evidently had an ill-fated love affair with either a woman or a man. Evidence for the latter is contained in "Live Oak with Moss," a cluster of poems he wrote in 1859 that traced a relationship that involved love, renunciation, and loss. These poems formed the basis of the homoerotic "Calamus" cluster, which appeared in the 1860 edition of *Leaves of Grass* and contained the lines: "(I loved a certain person ardently and my love was not return'd, / Yet out of that love I have written these songs.)"[57]

Whitman spent much of his time in the late 1850s with the crowd that gathered at Charles Pfaff's cellar restaurant-saloon on Broadway, just north of Bleecker Street. Headed by former abolitionist and free-lover Henry Clapp, the Pfaff bohemians consisted of arty, unconventional types, including actresses Ada Clare and Adah Isaacs Menken, who scandalized the respectable by flaunting their illicit love affairs; author Fitz-James O'Brien, who wrote Poesque horror stories; and humorist Artemus Ward. Whitman's "greatest pleasure" at Pfaff's, he would recall, was "to see, talk little, absorb" the lively repartee around him.[58] "Laugh on laughers!" he wrote in "The Two Vaults," his poem about Pfaff's. "Drink on drinkers! / Bandy and jest! / Toss the theme from one to another!"[59]

After the cool reception of the first two editions of *Leaves of Grass,* Whitman may have feared that his mission as cultural poet was in jeopardy, but he did not leave off writing poetry and in fact went forward with plans for a third edition. He still believed his poems could have wide cultural influence, and imagined flooding the market with "copious thousands of copies" of his volume.[60] In his notebook, he told himself, "You must become a force in the state—and a real and great force—just as real and great as the president and congress—greater than they."[61]

All this dreaming could have come to naught if he had not been approached by the energetic Boston publishers Thayer and Eldridge, who offered to publish his new edition and "sell a large number of copies" through "numberless Agents."[62] Whitman spent three months in Boston, from March through May 1860, overseeing the production of the third edition. When the book appeared in June, it contained 166 poems, 154 of them new. For the first time, the poems were arranged in clusters, among which were "Chants Democratic," focusing on society and politics, "Enfans d'Adam," on love between the sexes, and "Calamus," on comradeship and same-sex love. Handsomely printed and bound, the 1860 edition sold some 3,000 to 4,000 copies. The reviews were predominantly positive, although an outcry arose against the sex poems in "Enfans d'Adam." Thayer and Eldridge, despite its grandiose promises, fell into financial hard times and declared bankruptcy in January 1861.

For the next two years, Whitman scratched out a living as a freelance journalist, writing a series of articles on local topics for the *Brooklyn Daily Standard*. He was now living on Portland Avenue with his mother and his brothers Jesse, Edward, and Jeff, along with Jeff's wife and their daughter. His father had died in 1855; one sister, Mary, was married and lived in Greenport on eastern Long Island, and the other, Hannah, lived in Vermont with her artist husband, Charles Heyde. In 1861, his brother George had joined the Union forces under Colonel Edward Ferrero; over the next four years he would travel more than 20,000 miles as a soldier and serve in twenty-one engagements or sieges. It was mainly because of George that Walt got close to the war. On December 16, 1862, word came that George had been wounded at Fredricksburg. Walt immediately went south to Falmouth, where George's regiment was camped, to assess the wound, which turned out not to be serious. When, on December 28, Walt returned to Washington, he thought he might stay a few weeks. His stay, interrupted by periodic visits home, would last ten years.

To make ends meet, Whitman took on minor government jobs, first as a copyist for the army paymaster and then as a clerk in the Bureau of Indian Affairs. His main interest was serving as a volunteer nurse in the Washington war hospitals, of which there were about forty. He spent much of his spare time roaming the crowded hospitals, comforting the wounded soldiers, and distributing little gifts, often contributed by Brooklyn or Washington friends, such as fruit, candy, stationery, stamps, tobacco, and books. He made some 600 hospital visits in three years, seeing between 80,000 and 100,00 soldiers. He filled his notebook with graphic, compassionate descriptions of soldiers afflicted with every imaginable wound or malady, registering the experience in his poem "The Wound Dresser":

> To the long rows of cots up and down each side I return,
> To each and all one after another I draw near, not one do I miss,
> An attendant follows holding a tray, he carries a refuse pail,
> Soon to be fill'd with clotted rags and blood, emptied, and filled
>   again.[63]

He would later say that the Civil War was "the very centre, circumference, umbillicus of my whole career."[64] For him, the war purged America of many of the social ills that had troubled him in the prewar years. He likened it to a thunderstorm that cleared the atmosphere. It pulled together virtually all Americans, North and South, in a common action and a spirit of heroic self-sacrifice. It replaced murky debates about states' rights and slavery extension with the crystal-clear conflict of secession versus union. If he considered the three morally equivocal presidents before the war "our topmost warning and shame," he found in Abraham Lincoln a redeemer president, who embodied all the qualities he cherished.[65] Small wonder that when he poeticized the war he could sound like a rabid booster: "War! An arm'd race is advancing! The welcome for battle, no turning away; / War! Be it weeks, months, or years, an arm'd race is advancing to welcome it."[66]

Just as the war, in his view, brought out the heroism of Americans, so the assassination of Lincoln unified them in grief. In Washington, Whitman had often seen the president on the streets, looking ordinary but impressive on a gray horse or in an open barouche, escorted by mounted cavalry with sabers by their sides. "We have got so that we exchange bows, and very cordial ones," he wrote of Lincoln.[67] The murder of Lincoln by John Wilkes Booth in Ford's Theatre was for Whitman a tragic apotheosis. The overwhelming sorrow that engulfed the nation provided what he called "a cement to the whole people, subtler, more underlying, than any thing in written constitution, or courts or armies."[68] The assassination elicited four Whitman poems, including the ever-popular "O Captain! My Captain!" and the lyrically eulogistic "When Lilacs Last in the Dooryard Bloom'd."

Besides witnessing the war and its leaders, Whitman developed close friendships in Washington. He dined often at the home of the volatile abolitionist William Douglas O'Connor and his reform-minded wife, Nelly, where he had endless discussions with the journalists and government workers who gathered there. Through political contacts, O'Connor got Whitman his clerkship in the Indian bureau. When Whitman was fired from the post after it was discovered he had written sexually explicit poetry, O'Connor penned a vitriolic pamphlet, *The Good Gray Poet*, which excoriated Whitman's accusers and argued for the essential propriety of his verse. The phrase the "Good Gray Poet" stuck to Whitman thereafter, used by many who wanted to minimize the sexual themes of his poetry.

The war years also brought romantic attachments. Whitman had at least two brief heterosexual affairs, including one with a woman who called him "such a good bedfellow."[69] The war also made same-sex bonding, which was unselfconscious and widespread anyway in a time before sexual "types" were defined, a common part of public behavior. Whitman overtly displayed affection to his soldier/comrades, hugging and kissing them with what he called a spirit of "exquisite courtesy—man to man— . . . in the highest sense, *propriety—propriety*."[70] His longest, most ardent relationship was with a young streetcar conductor, Peter Doyle, whom he described as a "full-blooded everyday divinely generous working man: a hail-fellow-well met: a little too fond of his beer, now and then, and of the women maybe: but for the most part the salt of the earth."[71] Whitman could get emotionally riled over Doyle, as when he warned himself in his notebook to give up "*this* FEVERISH, FLUCTUATING, *useless*, UNDIG-NIFIED PURSUIT *of* [Doyle]."[72] To what extent his relationship with Doyle or other men accorded with modern homosexual practices is much debated. Whitman himself, when asked later if his comradely feelings verged on the sexual, branded these "morbid inferences" as "damnable"—although this denial has often been called a mere evasion.[73] Suffice it to say he had flings with women, but his main attraction was to young men.

In 1865, Whitman gathered his war poems in a volume called *Drum-Taps*, which, along with Melville's *Battle Pieces*, contains the finest poetry produced by the Civil War. Whitman wrote that this volume had "none of the perturbations of *Leaves of Grass*," and several reviewers noted with pleasure the patriotic tone of the war poems.[74] On the basis of *Drum-Taps*, Whitman's naturalist friend John Burroughs wrote the first detailed appreciation of the poet, *Notes on Walt Whitman as Poet and Person* (1867). Burroughs portrayed Whitman as an unjustly persecuted poet who had proven his virtue in the war hospitals and who was thoroughly respectable in his private behavior, a sanitized portrait that defined the poet among his growing coterie of supporters in the postwar years. Whitman helped promote this scrubbed image of himself. Although theoretically opposed to expurgation, he raised little objection when William Michael Rossetti issued a British edition of his poems that left out many of the sexual pieces. The new poems that Whitman wrote for the 1867 edition of *Leaves of Grass* lacked the aggressive egotism and eroticism of his earlier work.

In the late 1860s, Whitman clerked in the attorney general's office, continuing to write poetry and, increasingly, essays. When Thomas Carlyle published "Shooting Niagara," a vicious denunciation of democracy, Whitman defended the American system in magazine articles that he eventually refurbished as the pamphlet *Democratic Vistas* (1871). Conceding that politics and business in America were "saturated in corruption," he pointed to the heroism of the Civil War soldiers and increasing opportunities for women as examples of the nation's underlying health.[75] Whitman's own health, however, was fragile. During the war, he had suffered dizzy spells and heaviness of the head, early symptoms of the cerebral hemorrhage that struck him in 1873. The stroke left him partly paralyzed for the remaining nineteen years of his life. He had remained emotionally close to his mother during the war years, and when her health failed in May 1873 he rushed to Camden, New Jersey, where she was living with his brother George. Her death shortly after his arrival was a crushing blow.

He stayed on in Camden, living first with George and his family and then, in 1884, buying his own modest house at 328 Mickle Street. His passionate poems inspired the distant love of an English widow, Anne Gilchrist, who confessed her devotion by letter and traveled to America in 1876 only to find that her love was not reciprocated. New editions of *Leaves of Grass* appeared in 1870 (dated 1871), 1876, and 1881. The last edition, published in Boston by James R. Osgood, was attacked by the city's district attorney on the grounds that it violated laws banning "obscene literature."[76] Predictably, the banning aroused the public's curiosity, and when the 1881 edition was republished in Philadelphia, sales were brisk. Although he never became a bestselling poet, Whitman gained celebrity status. Among the many who traveled to Camden to meet him were Henry Wadsworth Longfellow, Edmund Gosse, and Oscar Wilde. Widely revered as the Good Gray Poet, he was often asked to give his patriotic lecture, "The Death of Abraham Lincoln." The lectures became big fundraising events; in New York in April 1887, for example, he earned $600 by lecturing before a crowd that included Andrew Carnegie, James Russell Lowell, and Mark Twain. A number of commercial products were named after him; there was even a Walt Whitman Cigar. A group of acolytes in Bolton, England, organized a church around his religious teachings, and Whitman societies sprang up as far away as Australia.

While he basked in this adulation, Whitman continued to live simply in his cramped, two-story frame house on Mickle Street, where his long-suffering housekeeper, Mary Davis, served him without pay for the last eight years of his life. After he suffered severe strokes in 1888, he was attended by a series of male nurses. He was visited almost daily by a young socialist friend, Horace Traubel, who wrote down their conversations in thick books that

24. *WEP*, 39–40.

25. Traubel et al., eds., *In Re Walt Whitman*, 33.

26. *TC*, I:39–40.

27. See, especially, Mark Summers, *The Plundering Generation: Corruption and the Crisis of the Union* (New York: Oxford University Press, 1987).

28. *WCP*, 18.

29. *LGC*, 52.

30. *DN*, III:736.

31. [A.S. Hill], *North American Review* 104 (Jan. 1867): 302; *New York Examiner*, January 9, 1882.

32. *PW*, II: 597.

33. *LGC*, 67. The next quotation is on 163.

34. *Brooklyn Star*, November 5, 1845.

35. Cleveland Rodgers and John Black, eds., *The Gathering of the Forces* (New York: G. P. Putnam's Sons, 1920), 346–47; Whitman, *Notes and Fragments*, ed. Richard Maurice Bucke (1899; rpt., Ontario: A. Talbot and co., n.d.), 70.

36. *Brooklyn Daily Eagle*, March 13, 1847.

37. *Variovum*, I:31.

38. John Townsend Trowbridge, *Atlantic Monthly* 89 (Feb. 1902): 166.

39. Clarence Gohdes and Rollo G. Silver, eds., *Faint Clews & Indirections: Manuscripts of Walt Whitman and His Family* (Durham, N.C.: Duke University Press, 1949), p. 19.

40. *LGC*, 56.

41. *NYD*, 127.

42. *NUPM*, IV:1604.

43. *I Sit* 113.

44. *WCP*, 19.

45. *LGC*, 1.

46. *WCP*, 26.

47. *LGC*, 729.

48. *CH*, 22.

49. *CH*, 32, 61.

50. *WCP*, 1327.

51. "By Blue Ontario's Shore," *LGC*, 351 (emphasis added).

52. Joel Myerson, ed., *Whitman in His Own Time* (Detroit: Omnigraphics, 1991), 334.

53. Walter Harding and Carl Bode, eds., *The Correspondence of Henry David Thoreau* (Westport, Conn.: Greenwood, 1974), 444.

54. *WWC*, I:212.

55. *NUPM*, I:1554.

56. *NUPM*, I:353.

57. *LGC*, 134.

58. *WWC*, I:417.

59. *LGC*, 660.

60. *New York Saturday Press*, January 7, 1860.

61. *NUPM*, I:417.

62. William Thayer and Charles Eldridge to Whitman, letter of February 10, 1860. Feinberg Collection, Library of Congress.

63. *LGC*, 310.

64. *WWC*, III:95.

65. *PW*, II:429.

66. "First O Songs for a Prelude," *LGC*, 281.

67. *PW*, I:60.

68. *PW*, II:508.

69. Peter Doyle to Whitman, letter of September 27, 1868. Morgan Library (New York).

70. *WWC*, IV:195.

71. *WWC*, III:543.

72. *NUPM*, II:888–89.

73. *TC*, V:72.

74. *TC*, I:247.

75. *PW*, II:370.

76. Oliver Stevens to James R. Osgood, letter of March 1, 1882. Feinberg Collection, Library of Congress.

WHITMAN IN
HIS TIME

Lucifer and Ethiopia

Whitman, Race, and Poetics before
the Civil War and After

Ed Folsom

It would perhaps be nice if Walt Whitman, our great poet of
American democracy, had possessed a spotless attitude toward
race in the United States and if he had clearly and unambiguously
espoused the equality of all individuals, regardless of race.[1] But
Whitman was a poet embedded in his times, and his times—not
unlike our own—were a period of intense disagreement about the
significance and importance of racial difference. His career demonstrates his struggle with his times—and with himself—over the
issue of race in the United States, and, because of that, his work
offers important insight into the ongoing struggle in America to
create a unified society that nonetheless maintains and celebrates
its diversity. One of the most instructive aspects of Whitman's poetry is its inscription of the distance and slippage between ideals
and reality. For all its lofty aspirations, Whitman's poetry is embedded in the messy pragmatics of compromise and equivoca-
tion, and, because of that, we can hear within it some of the tensions at the heart of American history.

The first three editions of *Leaves of Grass* (1855, 1856, 1860) appeared while slavery still existed in the United States; the final
three editions (1867, 1870–71, 1881) appeared after slavery was
abolished and during a time of social ferment about how the
freed slaves would be assimilated into American society. During

his career, Whitman's attitudes toward African Americans altered significantly. It is fair to say that he was more supportive of blacks during the period when the issue was slavery than during the period after emancipation, when the issue became the access of free blacks to the basic rights of citizenship, including the right to vote. For Whitman, as for many white Americans in the Civil War era, it was possible to be opposed to slavery but also to be against equal rights for African Americans.

In this essay, I investigate Whitman's complex and altering views about black Americans by focusing on two key figures in his poetry, the only two black characters to whom he gave voice in *Leaves of Grass*: "Lucifer," a young male slave who appears in Whitman's 1855 poem that he eventually named "The Sleepers," and "Ethiopia," an old female emancipated slave who appears in his 1870 poem "Ethiopia Saluting the Colors." Whitman incessantly shuffled and revised the contents of *Leaves of Grass* over the course of his career, and in one of his most surprising alterations, Lucifer vanishes from the final edition (1881) at just the moment that Ethiopia settles retroactively into "Drum-Taps," Whitman's cluster of Civil War poems. Whitman's manipulation of these two black figures is revealing, as the powerful and threatening enslaved young black man gives way to the ancient and ambiguous figure of the emancipated old black woman.

It has only been in the past few years, the last years of the twentieth century, that scholars have offered the first detailed examinations of Whitman's complex racial attitudes.[2] Over the course of his career, Whitman seems to have espoused the full spectrum of nineteenth-century white American racialist views. Recently, Martin Klammer has investigated in detail Whitman's shifting attitudes toward slavery leading up to and including the first edition of *Leaves*. Klammer traces Whitman's representations of blacks from his 1842 temperance novel, *Franklin Evans*, in which Klammer discerns proslavery attitudes, through his journalism, where Whitman develops a Free-Soil stance, accepting slavery where it then existed but unwilling to see it extended into developing territories and states in the West. Like many Free-Soilers, Whitman occasionally expressed his disdain for the extension of slavery, not out of concern for blacks but rather out of a desire to protect white labor from the degradation of having to compete with the forced free labor of black slaves. Klammer also finds, however, that in notebooks Whitman kept during the late 1840s and early 1850s, he developed a remarkable new set of experimental writings that reveal "a deeply humanitarian concern for the suffering of slaves" (*Whitman, Slavery, and the Emergence of "Leaves of Grass,"* 4), an attitude that permeates the first edition of *Leaves*. In the long poem that he would come to call "Song of Myself," Whitman embeds a slave escape narrative, with the narrator welcoming "the runaway slave" to his house and inviting him to "sit next me at table." Later, the narrator momentarily *becomes* "the hounded slave": "Hell and despair are upon me . . . / . . . they beat me violently over the head with their whip-stocks." The 1855 poem eventually known as "I Sing the Body Electric" focuses on a slave auction and deals with redefining the value of the black bodies that are sold; in his notes for arranging the original edition of *Leaves*, Whitman referred to this poem as "Slaves."[3] Most remarkably of all, in the poem later known as "The Sleepers," Whitman made the radical gesture of actually turning his narration over to an angry black slave, Lucifer, who, like his namesake, is an emblem of rebellion, a figure unafraid to confront the ultimate master.

Black Lucifer

Now Lucifer was not dead . . . or if he was I am his sorrowful
    terrible heir;
I have been wronged. . . . I am oppressed . . . I hate him that
    oppresses me,
I will either destroy him, or he shall release me.
Damn him! How he does defile me,
How he informs against my brother and sister and takes pay for
    their blood,
How he laughs when I look down the bend after the steamboat that
    carries away my woman.

Now the vast bulk that is the whale's bulk . . . it seems mine,
Warily, sportsman! Though I lie so sleepy and sluggish, my tap is
    death. (*WCP,* 113)

This brief but powerful passage has received some illuminating commentary in recent years, including Christopher Beach's interpretation of it in the context of surrounding social discourses that connected whales and slavery; the significance of the passage, Beach argues, is in "Whitman's creation of enabling figures for the slave's self-expression; Lucifer and the black whale . . . represent at once the slave's inability to speak within the system of dominant white discourses and Whitman's poetic attempt to give a voice to the slave" (*Politics of Distinction,* 93). It is a passage that Whitman worked hard on in various notes and drafts. In one early notebook, where Whitman combined slavery scenes that would later find their separate ways into "Song of Myself" and "The Sleepers," he wrote:

The hunted slave who flags in the race at last, and leans up by the
    fence, blowing and covered with sweat,
And the twinges that sting like needles his breast and neck
The murderous buck-shot and the bullets.
All this I not only feel and see but am.
I am the hunted slave

....

What the rebel felt gaily adjusting his neck to the rope noose,
What Lucifer cursed when tumbling from Heaven (*NUPM,* I:110)

In another early notebook, Whitman lists gods, including Lucifer, who are defined as "made up of all that opposes hinders, obstructs, revolts" (*NUPM,* VI:2025). And in another draft of an early poem, "Pictures," Whitman again ties Lucifer to blacks and to revolt.

And this black portrait—this head, huge, frowning, sorrowful,—is
    Lucifer's portrait—the denied God's portrait,
(But I do not deny him—though cast out and rebellious, he is my
God as much as any;). (*NUPM,* IV:1300)

Picking up on this image, Whitman drafts the Lucifer passage, using the name "Black Lucifer" (*LGC,* 628n): "Black Lucifer was not dead; . . . I am the God of revolt—deathless, sorrowful, vast" (*NUPM*, IV:1300–1301n). It is an intense and explosive conflation, this joining of the angry black slave and the rebellious angel. In combining them and in expressing sympathy for the resultant figure of rebellion ("I do not deny him"), Whitman creates an incendiary image, one that was particularly volatile in the mid-1850s. Slave revolts in the South—already numbering in the hundreds—were multiplying (in the year following the publication of this poem, there would be slave revolts in twelve states), and a racial war threatened, the very kind of war that John Brown would try to precipitate a couple of years later with his raid on Harpers Ferry.

It is significant, too, that one definition of Lucifer in mid–nineteenth-century dictionaries was "a match made of a sliver of wood tipped with a combustible substance, and ignited by friction." Easily ignitable matches had begun to be manufactured in the 1830s, and these portable instruments of friction and fire were also called "lucifer-matches" or "loco-focos" (a playful derivative of Latin, meaning "in place of fire" or "self-generated fire").[4] "Locofocos," of course, was the name given to the radical wing of the Democratic party (because in 1835 they used the newly invented matches to light candles when conservatives tried to silence them by turning out the gaslights in their convention hall); these radicals were adherents of William Leggett, who urged Locofocos to endorse an early and strong antislavery position. Underlying Whitman's choice of a name for his first slave character, then, was his own early admiration of the Locofocos and of Leggett's egalitarian program. Whitman's Lucifer was a "combustible substance," too, a lucifer-match flaming into an expression of hate and rage and threatening to turn his apparent sluggishness into a massive movement of death, a loco-foco slave ignited by a lifetime of friction with his cruel master and with the dehumanizing institution of slavery.

When this powerful figure of Lucifer flamed into speech in Whitman's poem, he became one of the earliest expressions of black subjectivity in a work by a white poet. He is the culmination of a voice Whitman was moving toward from his very earliest notes that anticipate the 1855 *Leaves*. In the notebook where we can

first see the stirrings of his radical new poetry, Whitman hesitat-
ingly inscribes a whole new kind of speaking, a wild attempt to
voice the full range of selves in his contradictory nation.

I am the poet of slaves and of the masters of slaves
I am the poet of the body
And I am

I am the poet of the body
And I am the poet of the soul
I go with the slaves of the earth equally with the masters
And I will stand between the masters and the slaves,
Entering into both so that both shall understand me alike. (*NUPM*,
    I:67)

This originating moment of *Leaves of Grass* has sparked a great
deal of commentary. If nothing else, it reveals that, at its incep-
tion, *Leaves* was not an "abolitionist" work, at least not in the conventional sense of that term, for in abolitionist works the slave is
pitied and the slave master demonized, and the irresolvable dichotomies of the nation are intensified. Whitman instead probes
for a voice that reconciles the dichotomies, one inclusive enough
to speak for slave and master—or one that negotiates the distance
between the two. This is the beginning of Whitman's attempt to
become that impossible representative American voice—the *fully*
representative voice—that speaks not for parties or factions but
for everyone in the nation, a voice fluid enough to inhabit the sub-
jectivities of all individuals in the culture. Whitman in these first
notes identifies the poles of human possibility—the spectrum his
capacious poetic voice would have to cover—as they appeared to
him at mid–nineteenth century: from slave to master of slaves.
His dawning insight had to do with a belief that each and every
democratic self was vast and contradictory, as variegated as
the nation itself, and so the poet had to awaken the nation, to
bring Americans out of their lethargy of discrimination and
hierarchy to understand that, within themselves, they potentially
contained—in fact, potentially *were*—everyone else. The end of
slavery would come, Whitman believed, when the slave owner

and the slave could both be represented by the same voice, could both hear themselves in the "I" and the "you" of the democratic poet, when the slave master could experience the potential slave within himself, and when the slave could know the master within himself, at which moment of illumination slavery would end. It was a spiritual and ontological abolition, a desperate attempt to present a unifying instead of a divisive voice, and by the time Whitman published this voice in 1855, the nation was only five years away from discovering how fully the forces of division and violence would overpower the fading hopes of unity and absorption of difference.

But, when he was writing his poem about Lucifer, Whitman's faith was still strong. First, however, he had to give voice to Lucifer's rage. In a draft, Whitman spells out the challenge: "I am a curse: a negro thinks me / You cannot speak yourself, negro / I dart like a snake from your mouth" (*LGC*, 628). Whitman works to turn his poem over to the consciousness and the sensibility of a black slave, allowing himself to be *thought* by "a negro" and then letting his voice emerge from the black slave's mouth. Whitman's attempt is not to speak *for* the black slave but to speak *as* the black slave, an act that, of course, hovers precariously between subjugation of the slave (who seems to be able to speak only when the white poet imagines himself speaking as a black slave) and full recognition of his subjectivity (the poet imagines himself inhabited by another, in fact, *inhabiting* another). Whether the poem enacts Whitman's domination of the slave or the slave's domination of Whitman—or some endless, tensed identity transfer—it remains one of the most powerful and evocative passages about slavery in American literature. By the time Whitman settled on the language for the published version of the passage, he had obliterated his own "I" and given the "I" over totally to Lucifer. The slave is *subject* instead of object here, and, unlike Whitman's postbellum black character Ethiopia, Lucifer has powerful access to his own subjectivity and agency ("I will either destroy him," he says of his white master, "or he shall release me").

But Lucifer's expression of hate and his vow of action against the slave master are not the final words in the poem. Whitman ends the poem with a vast, unifying catalog, a vision of the universe "duly in order . . . every thing is in its place." This absorptive vision includes, surprisingly, Lucifer now joined with his master, presumably after they have experienced the illumination of their oneness in an emerging democratic sensibility: "The call of the slave is one with the master's call . . . and the master salutes the slave" (*WCP*, 115–16). The image of Lucifer flaring into hatred and violent action is subsumed by the final image, which offers a resolution more exalted than violence and hate, a seemingly unlikely resolution of love, understanding, oneness, in which the slave owner now sees the error of his ways and joins voices with the slave, saluting him in some unspecified gesture of respect. Here, at the end of the poem that would become "The Sleepers," Whitman comes as close as he ever would to attaining the voice that would speak for the slaves and for the masters of slaves ("The diverse shall be no less diverse, but they shall flow and unite . . . they unite now"), but it is a voice that fails to alter the course of American history, and it is a voice that in no way begins to address what could, should, or would happen to black Americans after slavery's end.

The Lucifer passage lingers in *Leaves* through the first two postwar editions as a vestige of Whitman's antebellum desire to voice the subjectivity of the slave, to give the slave power and agency, and to imagine that that poetic act might be enough to change the slave master's perception of slaves, to coerce the slave masters to recognize the humanity in those they treated as objects and possessions, as less than human. But these desires were increasingly anachronistic: Lucifer's cry against slavery seemed less and less relevant to the postwar concerns of the nation, when Lucifer's cry had changed to a demand for citizenship and civil rights. Did Whitman's Lucifer go on, after emancipation, to become a citizen, to vote? The question seems faintly ridiculous, because Lucifer fails to evolve in Whitman's work; the poet creates no black characters, not a hint of a representation that offers a place or role for the freed slaves in reconstructed America. He toys with the idea of writing a "Poem of the Black Person," complete with "the sentiment of a sweeping, surrounding, shielding, protection of the blacks," but the poem never materializes.[5] He thinks of writing a "Poem of Remorse" in which he would "look back to the times when I thought others—slaves—the ignorant—so much inferior to myself / To have so much less right" (*DN*, 791). He writes a powerful journalistic piece, evoking "the slave trade" and describing the horrifying conditions on slave ships that had still been operating illegally in the late 1850s out of New York.[6] But Whitman adds no black figures to his poetry during the Civil War years. Then, suddenly, in 1867, he begins to work on a single new black character who would enter *Leaves of Grass* in 1870 and stay there after Lucifer vanishes in the final editions and last issues of Whitman's life's work. Readers opening the 1881 edition of *Leaves* to read "The Sleepers" found that Lucifer's voice—Whitman's brave and complex achievement, bound inextricably to the very origins of *Leaves*—had now gone silent.[7]

Whitman as Poet and Reconstructionist in 1867

During the summer of 1867—twelve years after the Lucifer passage was published and two years after the Civil War ended—Whitman wrote one of his strangest poems, "Ethiopia Saluting the Colors," a short work that over the years has generally been met with embarrassed silence. When it gets mentioned at all, the poem is usually cited as an example of how Whitman still occasionally employed conventional rhymes and meters.[8] We will look in some detail at the social origins and historical contexts of this odd poem. I view it as a kind of counter-emblem to the Lucifer passage, a charged cluster of words emerging out of a period of massive transition for both Whitman and the country, as both struggled to figure out how they would reconstruct their patterns of living after the Civil War, what ideals they would live by, and how the future of America would be redefined.

"Ethiopia Saluting the Colors"

Who are you dusky woman, so ancient hardly human,
With your woolly-white and turban'd head, and bare bony feet?
Why rising by the roadside here, do you the colors greet?

('Tis while our army lines Carolina's sands and pines,
Forth from thy hovel door thou Ethiopia com'st to me,
As under doughty Sherman I march toward the sea.)

Me master years a hundred since from my parents sunder'd,
A little child, they caught me as the savage beast is caught,
Then hither me across the sea the cruel slaver brought.

No further does she say, but lingering all the day,
Her high-borne turban'd head she wags, and rolls her darkling eye,
And courtesies to the regiments, the guidons moving by.

What is it fateful woman, so blear, hardly human?
Why wag your head with turban bound, yellow, red and green?
Are the things so strange and marvelous you see or have seen?
    (*LGC*, 318–19)

The remarkably intricate form of the poem, with its uncharacteristic internal and end rhyme, has already been analyzed
thoroughly.[9] What should be noted is that Whitman tended to
embrace conventional metric and rhyme schemes at times when
he felt acute social instability, as just after Lincoln's assassination,
when his organic poetics gave way temporarily to the extremely
patterned "O Captain! My Captain!" The repetitive stability and
predictability of conventional form sustained Whitman through
the initial phases of difficult times, offering him balance and cohesion when he most needed it. There were moments, both public and private, when his usual open form threatened to shatter
into fragments, when he needed the solace and the predictability
of patterned verse. (It is worth recalling that most of his
pre–*Leaves* verse was highly patterned and rhymed, that the very
foundation of his poetry writing was formal, and so convention
was an available retreat for Whitman.)[10] What social upheaval,
what cultural instability was Whitman facing in 1867 that might
have sent him once again to such a tightly structured pattern, ar-
guably the most patterned poem he ever wrote?

Let's first recall what we know about the history of the poem,
for Whitman certainly seemed more anxious about the fate of
this poem than he was about any other poems around this time.

On September 7, 1867, he submitted a poem he then called "Ethiopia Commenting" to the Church brothers at the *Galaxy* magazine and asked $25 for it. In the same letter, he let the Churches know he was also in the midst of writing a lengthy article "partly provoked by, & in some respects a rejoinder to, Carlyle's *Shooting Niagara*" (*TC,* I:337–38). Francis P. Church accepted the poem but wanted to "keep it back" until after the *Galaxy* published Whitman's "Democracy" essay, the first part of what would eventually become *Democratic Vistas* (see *TC,* I:341–43). "Democracy" was published in the December issue, and, by December 30, Whitman was beginning to worry about not yet having seen proofs of the poem (*TC,* I:354). By the following March, he was still pressuring the Churches to publish the poem immediately (*TC,* II:21), and on November 2, 1868, frustrated by the Churches' puzzling silence about the poem, Whitman withdrew it from the *Galaxy* and claimed to submit it elsewhere (*TC,* II:69). Meanwhile, the second part of Whitman's *Democratic Vistas,* "Personalism," had been published in the *Galaxy* (May 1868), and his plans to publish a third part, to be called "Orbic Literature," were dashed when the Churches, who had apparently had enough of Whitman's haranguing prophecies about America's future, decided that two parts were enough (*TC,* II:31–33).

Drum-Taps and *Sequel to Drum-Taps* had been published in 1865, and Whitman had entered his long postwar period of significantly reduced poetic activity. Just as the nation entered into a long period of Reconstruction, so Whitman began to devote his energies to the poetic reconstruction of *Leaves of Grass,* incorporating *Drum-Taps* into *Leaves* and beginning the fifteen-year process of arranging and rearranging his poems to restructure the overall pattern of his book. "The reconstruction of the nation during and after the war years," writes Betsy Erkkila, "began for Whitman with the act of reconstructing his poems" (*Political Poet,* 260). "Ethiopia Saluting the Colors" would become a key element in his radical poetic reconstruction, for eventually he would incorporate it into his final (1881) version of "Drum-Taps," thus inserting a volatile issue—the role of blacks in America's future—into his group of Civil War poems in which he had, to that point, studiously avoided any comment on the topic. The Emancipation Proclamation had come and gone without Whitman even commenting on it, at least not in any documents that remain, and his Civil War poems never even suggested that slavery was an issue in the war.

The year 1867, then, was liminal for Whitman, as it was for the nation; it was the year of birth pangs issuing from the death pangs of the Civil War. The United States was reconstructing itself—becoming a singular instead of a plural noun—but the shape of the new nation was uncertain, as malleable as the intense debates and shifting votes of a Congress that was revising the very Constitution and threatening to impeach the president. Whitman, during this time, continued to visit the Civil War hospitals, which, two years after the war had ended, remained open, still filled with wounded soldiers (see *TC*, I:331; *TC*, I:275–76). Some nights he spent at the bedsides of these soldiers, and others he spent at the Capitol, watching the extraordinary night sessions with their momentous debates on Reconstruction legislation, just as the year before he had watched the debates on the Fourteenth Amendment (see *TC*, I: 277). "I went up to the Capitol Sunday night—Congress was in full blast in both houses— . . . the Radicals have passed their principal measures over the President's vetos— . . . There is much talk about impeachment—" (*TC*, I:316). He also attended the trial of John Surratt, who was charged with taking part in the assassination of Lincoln (*TC*, I:334).

The hospitals and the trial pulled Whitman to the past, to the war and the assassination that the nation was trying to forget, and the congressional debates pulled him to a confused future, in which the only thing that was clear was that the country was going to be something far different than it had been before. There was a sense in Washington that year that Congress was actually *creating* whatever it was that the war had been fought for. There was a widespread impression that the ideals espoused by Congress were in a sense retroactive, postwar articulations that were now being touted as the real reasons that the war had been fought. And, for the Radical Republicans, who controlled Congress, the war increasingly seemed to have been fought not just to emancipate the slaves (the Thirteenth Amendment had taken care of that) but to enfranchise them and guarantee them equal

rights under the Constitution. (This was the arena of the Fourteenth and Fifteenth amendments, and the amazing debates
dealt with the tricky issues of trying to unwrite the constitutional
provision that a slave counted as only three-fifths of a person and
trying to inscribe just what the black person's newly granted, full
humanity meant.)

The role of blacks in a reconstructed America was the focus of debate across the land, and it was an issue with which
Whitman—like most white Americans—was uncomfortable and
unsure. He began with high hopes. At the end of the war, Whitman made note of the abrupt appearance of blacks on Washington's streets; on the day of Lincoln's second inauguration, he
wrote of "the show" along Pennsylvania Avenue, where there
were "any quantity of male and female Africans, (especially female;)" and where "a regiment of blacks, in full uniform, with
guns on their shoulders" marched. He noted that every corner
had "its little squad" of people, "often soldiers, often black, with
raised faces, well worth looking at themselves, as new styles of
physiognomical pictures." Blacks at this point easily fit into Whitman's vision of a variegated postwar America: "The effect was
heterogeneous, novel, and quite inspiriting," he said, and, like
Whitman's vision of the democratic country itself, "Pennsylvania avenue absorbed all."[11] Whitman at this time celebrated the
emergence into cultural visibility of American blacks: Frederick
Douglass attended Lincoln's inaugural reception, and that year
blacks were for the first time allowed to attend White House social functions. In 1864, blacks were permitted in congressional
galleries, where they cheered the passage of the Thirteenth
Amendment.[12]

But, by the mid-1870s, when Whitman incorporated his inaugural description into *Memoranda During the War* and later into
Specimen Days, he simply dropped all references to blacks; by
then, the inauguration had come to be for Whitman an all-white
affair (see *PW*, I:92–96). At the same time that he was making the
decision to drop the Lucifer passage from "The Sleepers," then,
he was making analogous deletions in his published prose, drop-
ping all references to young and energetic blacks. Such blacks on
the streets of the capital had become a common sight in the

years following the inauguration, and each time Whitman noted the phenomenon, he found it less "inspiriting," as his fond hope for easy and quick national absorption of blacks gave way to a painful awareness of irreconcilable difference.

While attending the debates that were deciding the extent to which blacks would be allowed entry into the nation, Whitman looked at the changed world about him: "We had the greatest black procession here last Thursday—I didn't think there was so many darkeys, (especially wenches,) in the world—it was the anniversary of emancipation in this District" (*TC*, I:273–74). As African Americans took to the streets more and more frequently, Whitman responded with some disdain and a touch of fear and tried to reduce it all to a joke: "Washington is filled with *darkies*—the men & children & wenches swarm in all directions—(I am not sure but the North is like the man that won the elephant in a raffle)" (*TC*, I:323). The Union had won the big prize but now it had to figure out how to take care of "the beast" that accompanied the winner home. Whitman made that comment in early April 1867, within days of the first newspaper reports about the activities and beliefs of a new organization that had emerged in the South, which called itsaelf the Ku Klux Klan. By the following June, after blacks had exercised their newly won right to vote in the District of Columbia, Whitman's fear had intensified to alarm:

> We had the strangest procession here last Tuesday night, about 3000 darkeys, old & young, men & women—I saw them all—they turned out in honor of *their* victory in electing the Mayor, Mr. Bowen—the men were all armed with clubs or pistols—besides the procession in the street, there was a string went along the sidewalk in single file with bludgeons & sticks, yelling & gesticulating like madmen—it was quite comical, yet very disgusting & alarming in some respects—They were very insolent, & altogether it was a strange sight—they looked like so many wild brutes let loose—thousands of slaves from the Southern plantations have crowded up here—many are supported by the Gov't. (*TC*, II:34–35)

It hardly needs mentioning that Whitman's imagery follows familiar patterns of nineteenth-century racist stereotyping: blacks
are compared to "wild brutes," and the elephant joke underscores
the jungle animal associations; black women are "wenches" (in
nineteenth-century usage, a term for black female servants and
for women of "ill fame"), and the behavior of blacks is perceived
as insane—they "swarm" like insects (an image he would resur-
rect later to describe the black "Exodusters" who migrated to the
prairies [*NUPM*, III:1021]). Whitman can finally describe the overall experience only as "strange." Two years earlier, at Lincoln's inauguration, the parade of armed blacks was inspiring; now, out of
uniform and stripped of military control, the armed procession
had become comical, disgusting, and alarming.

It was at this time that Whitman inscribed in "Ethiopia" his
discomfort at being confronted with freed slaves who behaved
oddly, and his representation of his dis-ease took the form of a
monologue written by one of Sherman's soldiers, who had been
among the first northern whites accosted by exuberant "swarms"
of emancipated slaves.

Ethiopia in the American Consciousness in 1867

One question that never gets asked, but should, is: why did Whitman choose "Ethiopia" as the name of the saluter of the colors?
Ethiopia is the name, of course, of an African country, but no
American slaves came from Ethiopia (where the thriving slave
trade was directed instead toward the Middle East, supplying Arabic countries with slaves). "Africa" saluting the colors
would have made some sense, as would names like "Guinea" or
"Senegambia," where many American slaves originated; Whitman taught himself African geography and made careful notes
about the names and locations of these and other African countries and regions (*NUPM*, V:1971–72). But Ethiopia seems remarkably inappropriate, since it is an area of Africa that was not a
source of slaves for American consumption.

"Ethiopians," though, or the more common, shortened form

of the name, "Ethiops," had in the Western world by the mid–nineteenth century become synonymous with "Africans." German comparative anatomist Johann Friedrich Blumenbach had, around the turn of the nineteenth century, divided humankind into five families—white, yellow, brown, black, and red—and named the black family "Ethiopian."[13] Blumenbach's nomenclature became so generally accepted in studies of race that, even in an 1864 travel book by a white anthropologist about his journey to West Africa, the author uses the term "Ethiopic character" to describe the traits of the natives of Sierra Leone.[14] At least one widely reprinted mid–nineteenth-century map of Africa labeled the entire continent "Ethiopia," emblazoning the name from east coast to west and calling the southern Atlantic the "Ethiopic Ocean." [15]

If Whitman's title were "An Ethiop Saluting the Colors," then, we could hear the reference simply as a common appellation for any black: "Ethiopia" derives from the Greek for "burnt faces," and the term has been used since classical times to refer to blacks.[16] Whitman, early in his career, used the term in just such reductive and stereotypical ways, as when, in 1851, he admired William Sidney Mount's painting "of a Long Island negro" who had "a character of Americanism" But Whitman went on to object to "the exemplifying of our national attributes with Ethiopian minstrelsy,"[17] as if to suggest that Mount's admirable American figure would somehow have been more effective stripped of its deceptive blackface. (Whitman in the 1840s had been fond of a group of blackface singers called the "Ethiopian Serenaders.")[18] So, if Whitman had chosen to title his poem "An Ethiop Saluting the Colors," he would simply have been representing an expected racist term for the slave woman: it would have made sense that one of Sherman's soldiers—all 62,000 of whom were white—would have dismissed the old woman as an "Ethiop."

But Whitman instead insists on the *nation's* name. One critic assumes that "Ethiopia" is actually the slave woman's name and that the name is also a generic one that "applied to Negroes of the Southern United States in the nineteenth century."[19] But there is no evidence that the country name (as opposed to

"Ethiop" or "Ethiopian") was generally used this way.[20] In fact, Whitman's choice of the country's name suggests far more than a generic racial term. By the mid-1850s, Whitman, given his fascination with Egyptology, knew something about the history of Ethiopian culture, which was often portrayed as the seedbed of Egyptian culture. From Dr. Henry Abbott, proprietor of New York's Museum of Egyptian Antiquities (which Whitman visited often in the year or two before the first edition of *Leaves of Grass* was published), he learned of ancient Persians "finding monuments . . . with inscriptions and astronomical signs upon them" in Ethiopia (*NUPM*, I:138), and he found that "some antiquaries think the pyramids of Ethiopia the most ancient artificial structures now on the face of the globe"; the country seemed to contain the distant origins of civilization itself.[21] In his 1856 "Broad-Axe Poem," Whitman descends through a layering of cultures, down through the Greeks, Hebrews, Persians, Goths, Celts, arriving finally at the bedrock: "before any of those the venerable and harmless men of Ethiopia" (*LGC*, 184).[22] Whitman thus associates Ethiopia more with its biblical heritage, and he would have been aware of Frederick Douglass's stirring evocation—at the end of his 1852 speech "What to the Slave Is the Fourth of July?"—of Psalm 68:31: "There are forces in operation, which must inevitably work the downfall of slavery. . . . *Africa must rise and put on her yet unwoven garment. 'Ethiopia shall stretch out her hand unto God.'"*[23] Here, Ethiopia is again representative of all of black Africa and is appropriated by Douglass as a positive and spiritually charged appellation.

In "Ethiopia Saluting the Colors," then, the current displaced and degraded embodiment of Ethiopia—wearing Ethiopia's traditional flag colors (yellow, red, green) on her "high-borne turban'd head"—stands amazed and awed before a new mystery: an American flag that purports to liberate her from a long history of enslavement. Her head is not only borne high in pride for an ancient history she still contains, wears, and pays obeisance to, but Whitman's pun allows us to hear her as "high-born," born into a rich cultural tradition that those who see her in her current "hovel" with her "bare bony feet" cannot fathom. Ethiopia, in fact, is the only ancient state in Africa, the only nation that managed, as Sven Rubenson points out, to preserve "its independence throughout the era of European colonization,"[24] the one African country that never succumbed to European domination.

This rich past could no longer easily be imagined, because by the time of the American Civil War, Ethiopia was for most Americans a forgotten country, identified by those who knew of it at all as an ancient civilization that had declined over the centuries into a mysterious country of warring tribes.[25] In the eighteenth century, Abyssinia (as Europeans and Americans usually referred to the country) was still the stuff of romantic legend: Samuel Johnson's *History of Rasselas, Prince of Abissinia* was published in 1759, and James Bruce's famous *Travels to Discover the Source of the Nile* appeared in 1790 (and inspired Coleridge's image of "an Abyssinian maid" who "on her dulcimer . . . played" in his 1816 poem, "Kubla Khan").[26] Whitman's own mid-1850s notes suggest how distant this romantic Ethiopia had become: "Ethiopians," he notes, come from "a country doubtless of hot-breathed airs and exhalations cities, ignorance, altogether unenlightened and unexplored" (*NUPM*, V:1972).[27]

Whitman's pre–Civil War composite impression of Ethiopians, then, was of an ancient and accomplished people, the originators of civilization, who were now inscrutable and unenlightened but still fine physical specimens. This ambivalent impression is captured in "Ethiopia Saluting" by the soldier/narrator's characterization of the slave woman as "so ancient hardly human." The soldier senses something both ancient (as opposed to "primitive") and noble (her "high-borne turban'd head") about her at the same time that he perceives her to be savage (her "bare bony feet"), animal-like (her "woolly-white" hair, the way she "wags" her head, the way she was caught "as the savage beast is caught"), and unknowable (she is seen as a "fateful woman" who provokes unanswerable questions about "strange and marvelous" things). The soldier's description is filled with blurring terminology: the woman is "dusky" and "blear," always just out of focus.

In American newspapers in 1867 and 1868, Ethiopia was very much a dusky and blear country, but one that happened to be, for the first time, on the front pages. An international incident had been brewing in Ethiopia since early in 1864, when the Ethiopian emperor imprisoned the British consul, in part because Queen Victoria had insulted him by neglecting to answer his letter to her asking for an Ethiopian embassy in London.

The significant background of the incident is that, in 1855, a few months before *Leaves of Grass* appeared, a major event took place in Ethiopia, one that would remain obscure to Americans for many years. Kasa, a well-educated Christian patriot, who was almost exactly Whitman's age, culminated a long military campaign and was crowned "king of kings," the emperor of Ethiopia. Taking the name of Tewodros II (harking back to a legendary fifteenth-century emperor) and known in Europe as Theodore or Theodorus, he began a remarkable reign that would last more than a decade. A kind of Lincoln figure for Ethiopia, Tewodros worked to end a long civil war in his country, reunify it, abolish the slave trade, and usher the nation into the modern age. To help accomplish the latter objective, he approached Queen Victoria with a request to set up diplomatic relations with Britain. Victoria's failure to respond to Tewodros's letter led to his seizing of the British consul in Ethiopia. In a scenario not unlike some that have occurred more recently in U.S. history, Tewodros denied that he was holding the consul and staff hostage, claiming instead that they were his guests of state but that they were not free to leave. These guests were held in chains, and Victoria eventually sent another emissary to negotiate their release. After an apparently successful negotiation, Tewodros summarily imprisoned the second group along with the first just as they were ready to leave Ethiopia in the spring of 1866. During the summer that Whitman was writing his "Ethiopia" poem, Britain decided to send a military expedition to Ethiopia to secure the release of the hostages. Reports of this expedition regularly filled America's newspapers right up through the successful assault on the emperor's stronghold of Magdala, which resulted in the rescue of the hostages and the suicide of Tewodros, who shot himself with a pistol given to him by Victoria (and whose young son was taken to England to be educated at Rugby). Tewodros was almost immediately transformed into a legendary hero in Ethiopia, the subject of ballads still heard today, and Ethiopia returned to years of civil war and anarchy.

It was therefore during the summer of 1867, when Britain began its military incursion into Ethiopia, that the country first came to the attention of Americans, and Tewodros became a figure of international interest, a young and well-educated black African leader who had unified a country torn by civil war and who had taken steps to end slavery in his country. In the United States, the comparison to Lincoln was inevitable. Before 1867, Ethiopia was an unknown land; the *American Annual Cyclopaedia* for 1866 opened its discussion of the Ethiopian situation by noting "our little acquaintance with this country," while in the 1868 volume, it was noted that "the difficulty between England and King Theodore of Abyssinia, during the past three years, directed the special attention of the civilized world . . . to the affairs of this country."[28] By 1870, the country was quickly fading from the world's attention and memory: Ethiopia has "relapsed into entire obscurity," the *American Cyclopaedia* noted that year, "neither its relations to foreign countries nor its internal condition attracting the least attention" (*American Cyclopaedia*, 1870, 1). Ethiopia would in 1868 be forced to salute some foreign colors—the Union Jack—but in 1867, Tewodros had responded to the British threat with self-assurance and firm resistance ("Let them come," he said, in May 1867. "By the power of God I will meet them, and you may call me a woman if I do not beat them" [*American Cyclopaedia*, 1867, 2]). In Whitman's poem, then, the slave woman's ancient pride in her country— her sartorial salute to Ethiopia's colors—is appropriate and would have made a good deal of sense at the time. Ethiopia— the real country and the degraded embodiment of the rich heritage that the country represented—was emerging from a long period of degradation and gaining some dignity, respect, and freedom.

And the news from Ethiopia in 1867 and 1868 played into the domestic news in America: Tewodros's charismatic leadership and his tough talk to mighty Britain hardly fit the racialist stereotype of the docile black that was so often being described in the congressional debates on Reconstruction that Whitman spent his evenings attending.

Whitman and Ancient Black Women

"Ethiopia Saluting the Colors" would be a much different poem, then, if the freed slave had been portrayed as, say, a young man, as Black Lucifer finally freed from his chains (or as a proud Tewodros figure confronting colonial powers). A young black man rising to salute the U.S. colors would have been a more politically charged image. Questions of suffrage and of paternity and of amalgamation would have entered into the formula of the poem, all questions that were blazing issues in 1867 but issues about which Whitman experienced paralyzing ambivalence. An ancient black woman, however, was a safe representation. The whole issue of universal suffrage was being widely discussed, and the nascent women's movement in the United States had begun its rancorous separation from the movement for black citizenship (many early feminist leaders were furious about how the Fourteenth Amendment had written into the Constitution for the first time *male* privilege by punishing states that denied males the right to vote). But it was clear to everyone that women's suffrage was a long way down the road. A woman saluting the flag formed a more muted and conditioned act, a safer gesture, especially when that woman was clearly associated in Whitman's mind with a maternal, nurturing, but no longer fertile image. Whitman often praised large, old, black women. They recur in his stable of representations as far back as 1845, when, in his sketches called "Some Fact-Romances," he recalls "an aged black widow-woman" living in a basement in Manhattan; "the old creature . . . this ancient female," Whitman writes, "had no child, or any near relative; but was quite alone in the world" yet still "was remarkable every where for her agreeable ways and good humor—and all this at an age closely bordering on seventy" (*WEP*, 321). In 1848, in New Orleans, Whitman recalled that he started his days with a "large cup of delicious coffee . . . from the immense shining copper kettle of a great Creole mulatto woman (I believe she weigh'd 230 pounds)" (*PW*, II:606). In an 1862 article for the *New York Leader* on the Broadway Hospital, Whitman singles out "Aunty Robinson, a colored nurse" for particular praise; she reminds him of a "Southern *mammy*."

> She has big old-fashioned gold ear-rings in her ears, and wears a clear, bright red and yellow blue handkerchief around her head, and such an expression on her face, that I at once made up my mind, if ever I should be unfortunate enough to go to the Hospital as a patient, I should want to be nursed by Aunty Robinson. [29]

In the "Ethiopia" poem, Aunty Robinson's red, yellow, and blue handkerchief has been transmuted into a turban in Ethiopia's colors of red, yellow, and green, but she is the same familiarly exotic "mammy" who had comforted Whitman on and off for more than twenty years before she rose up by the roadside in his Reconstruction poem, as old as the Creole woman was large. Whitman would always harbor this desire to be nursed by an old black woman. In 1882, when he published *Specimen Days*, he was still pushing his dream, recalling his hospital days in Washington: "There are plenty of excellent clean old black women that would make tip-top nurses" (*PW*, I:88).

So the old woman of the poem is a conflation of Whitman's long-desired black maternal nurse, nonthreatening and accommodating, an Aunty Robinson in a hovel. In Whitman's hands, she is the sought-after, postwar, emblematic black for white America: puzzling in her origins, submissive in her courtesy, insistent in her salute, a person with shared and perhaps divided loyalties to her African past and to her American future, she experiences now a dual dispossession.

Whitman, of course, was not the only writer to cast the postwar black as an old woman who somehow meant something fateful for the reconstructed nation. Herman Melville, in *Battle-Pieces* (in 1866, the year before Whitman began work on his poem), offers his own rhymed emblematic poem, "Formerly a Slave," based on a drawing by American artist Elihu Vedder. Like Whitman's Ethiopia, Melville's old black woman gets her freedom too late to do much good for herself, but she nonetheless represents a vague, prophetic hope for the future, just as she also represents the ancient, thousand-year depths of civilization.

The sufferance of her race is shown,
    And retrospect of life,
Which now too late deliverance dawns upon;
    Yet is she not at strife.

Her children's children they shall know
    The good withheld from her;
And so her reverie takes prophetic cheer—
    In spirit she sees the stir

Far down the depth of thousand years,
    And marks the revel shine;
Her dusky face is lit with sober light,
    Sibylline, yet benign.[30]

This benign sybil was based, according to Vedder, on Jane Jackson, "an old negro woman [who] sold peanuts" near Vedder's studio in Manhattan: "She had been a slave down South, and had at that time a son . . . fighting in the Union Army."[31] Vedder sketched her, then painted her portrait, and later used her face as the basis for his well-known painting of the *Cumean Sibyl* (see p. 243). Though she has not before been suggested as a model for Whitman's Ethiopia, it is noteworthy that Whitman did know Vedder—they had been friends at Pfaff's beer hall in the early years of the war (see *NUPM*, I:468; Vedder, 218)—and he may well have seen Vedder's drawing, as well as have read Melville's poem. Certainly his portrayal of the "ancient," "turban'd," and "fateful" woman echoes Vedder's and Melville's old woman.

Unlike Melville's slave woman, however, Whitman's Ethiopia actually is given voice. Like Black Lucifer, she speaks, but her words are far different from the angry slave in "The Sleepers," whose striking presence derives precisely from his powerful expression of agency: he speaks a full subjectivity out of his enslavement, and his "I," displacing Whitman's narrator's "I," is clear and strong. Ethiopia, on the other hand, literally cannot speak an "I." Her voice is all *object* instead of subject—*"Me master years a hundred since from my parents sunder'd"*—and her self is defined by its being acted upon rather than acting. Her grammar, restricted to a passive voice, echoes a life out of her control. In this poem, as she approaches the soldier, she is perhaps taking her first step into active identity after a long lifetime of being sundered, caught, brought, and bought. Her posture is the opposite of Lucifer's; she is as passive and courteous as he is aggressive and vengeful. Ethiopia now looks to the confused soldier/narrator as the next person to guide her out of her object-hood and into her selfhood.[32]

"Cold-Blooded Sherman"

It is important to note that this poem is uncharacteristic of Whitman in more ways than its patterned rhyme and meter. Ethiopia speaks in this poem but only within the framing voice of another speaker, a distinct persona, an "I" that is clearly different from Whitman's typical fluid and absorbing "I." Whitman's usual "I" may be far from an autobiographical voice, but it is generally identifiable as the poet's voice, unlike the speaker of "Ethiopia." There is no other single poem in all of *Leaves* that is so clearly spoken by a fictionalized character, in such a carefully defined time and place. This persona is a soldier in Sherman's army, somewhere in the Carolinas, on the famous "march to the sea." Sherman's march to the sea, however, culminated in Savannah in late 1864, and in early 1865 he turned north to punish North Carolina, the state that started the Civil War; at that point, of course, he was no longer marching to the sea. The complications proliferate when we consider the subtitle that Whitman furnished for the poem in 1871, "A Reminiscence of 1864," which gives the incorrect year, since the Carolina campaign did not start until well into 1865. This confusion is not the only one in the poem, but it is difficult to know whether the confusion is Whitman's or whether Whitman inscribes the mistake as a revealing trait of the soldier/narrator, who is not quite sure where he is or why he's doing what he's doing. It is clear that the soldier persona is not sure why the black woman is saluting the American colors, even though he supposedly is part of the emancipating force. His general ignorance and confusion can be read as Whitman's commentary on the soldier's blind obedience to Sherman's high command and as a more general comment on the soldier's (and the country's) uncertainty about the motivations for and purposes of the war. If it was a war to free the slaves, as more and more northerners were claiming by 1866, then, Whitman suggests, the soldiers themselves were not always aware of that fact.

Whitman sets his poem, then, in the birthplace of the Civil War at the historical moment of retribution. Sherman's march through South Carolina was generally perceived as the Union's great revenge: "Here is where treason began," said one of the soldiers, "and, by God, here is where it shall end" (McPherson, *Battle Cry of Freedom,* 826). South Carolina "sowed the Wind," warned an Iowa soldier. "She shall soon reap the Whirlwind."[33] This was the march through swamps that "cold-blooded Sherman," as Whitman called him,[34] said was his most difficult maneuver but also finally his most devastating; in comparison, he said, the march to the sea was "child's play" (McPherson, *Battle Cry of Freedom,* 827).

Sherman's soldiers were—with the exception of one marginalized black regiment that joined the force at Savannah and that was used exclusively for clearing roads and guarding hospitals (Glatthaar, *March to the Sea,* 57)—an all-white outfit. They were mostly westerners who had had few encounters with blacks until they met the thousands of freedmen who flocked to the army and marched with it (10,000 slaves accompanied the army to Savannah, another 7,000 to Fayetteville, North Carolina). While some of the troops saw their mission as abolitionist in nature and strongly supported the Emancipation Proclamation, most of the soldiers harbored deep racial hatred and, as historian Joseph Glatthaar has noted, "found blacks a nuisance and vented their prejudices and wartime frustrations on the black race" (*March to the Sea,* 52). The soldiers were out to preserve the Union and punish the secessionists, and, like much of the rest of the North (including Whitman and Lincoln for most of the war), they did not see the purpose of the war as the freeing of slaves. One Union soldier's exclamation—"Fight for the nigger! I'd see 'em in de bottom of a swamp before I'd fight for 'em" (Glatthaar, *March to the Sea,* 40)—was indicative of a widespread attitude. There are records of countless abuses (including murders) of freed slaves by Sherman's troops, culminating on the march to Savannah when the Fourteenth Corps (commanded by a Union officer named Jefferson Davis!) laid down a pontoon bridge to cross a deep creek as they were fleeing Confederate cavalry. The bridge was taken up before the hundreds of accompanying blacks could use it, leaving the terrified freed slaves to swim for their lives. Many drowned, while others were killed by Confederate guerrillas. "Where can you find in all the annals of plantation cruelty," wrote one Union private, "anything more completely inhuman and fiendish than this?" (Glatthaar, *March to the Sea,* 64).

It was common for the slaves who latched onto Sherman's troops to discuss at length with the soldiers the evils of slavery and to treat the Union soldiers as saviors. The scene that Whitman portrays in his poem is one that was, in some form, repeated many times.[35] One soldier recalled that "all along the way, Negroes swarmed out to greet the blue-coated soldiers, hailing them as if they were delivering angels," and prominent among the blacks who "streamed to march along with the advancing soldiers" were "white-haired household slaves" who "limped with weariness along the dusty road."[36] In one incident analogous to the moment recorded by Whitman, a large slave woman hugged a soldier and loudly announced, "We'uns done heered dis wuz an army ob debils fum hell, but praise de Lawd, praise de Lawd, it's de Lawd's own babes an sucklin's!" (Glatthaar, *March to the Sea,*62).

Whitman's narrator, then, would have been a part of this battle-weary, elite group of western soldiers, whose opinions about the freed slaves ran the gamut but were usually, at least early in the march, racist and dismissive. One of the first stops that Sherman's troops made after leaving Savannah was Beaufort, South Carolina, part of the Port Royal Experiment, a federal project to create an autonomous black community. The success of the experiment galled many of the soldiers, who believed the relatively prosperous blacks that they saw in Beaufort were getting preferential treatment and were faring better than the soldiers. But for many of the soldiers, exposure to freed blacks served to undermine their initial racist assumptions, and they came to admire the former slaves as a lively and intelligent people. One officer wrote near the end of the campaign: "The more we become acquainted with the negro character, both as men and Christians, the more we are compelled to respect them" (Glatthaar, *March to the Sea,* 65). The reformed attitude of one Indiana soldier suggests both his newly won respect for blacks and his growing anxiety about the future of freedmen: "It is depressing to see their joy, when one thinks of the impossibility of their attaining their ideal of freedom. . . . We laugh now at their wild antics, and marvelous expectations, but cannot shut out the thought that the comedy may soon darken into tragedy" (Glatthaar, *March to the Sea,* 178).

Whitman's soldier/narrator, then, was typical of most of the soldiers in Sherman's army, confused about their relationship to the blacks who saw them as their emancipators, ambivalent about sharing freedom with the slaves, curious about the inexplicable gestures of defiance, hope, and joy that these newly freed people made in the presence of Sherman's troops. It is crucial to emphasize what most readers of the poem ignore: that it is narrated by a soldier, and it is *his* view of the old black woman that is "dusky" and "blear."[37] The woman herself is as clear as she can be; his response to her is what is hard to get in focus. He is not sure what his purpose is, so he has trouble understanding her salute to him. She is far more aware of what he represents in American history than he is.

Whitman created his narrator out of his personal encounters with soldiers who experienced the march through "Carolina's sands and pines," memorable landscapes for Sherman's soldiers, one of whom described what he saw on the march in this way: "Negroes, white sand, and scrub pine constitutes what I have seen of North Carolina."[38] Sherman himself once told the *Harper's* artists accompanying him that they needed to send only one picture back to New York to represent "all South Carolina"—"one big pine tree, one log cabin, and one nigger."[39] Whitman built his narrator's experiences—sands, pines, the black woman, and the hovel—from accounts he heard from soldiers when he talked to them upon their return to Washington in May 1865. He had been following their movements closely, monitoring their responses to the major events of the day.

> When Sherman's armies, (long after they left Atlanta,) were marching through South and North Carolina—after leaving Savannah, the news of Lee's capitulation having been receiv'd—the men never mov'd a mile without from some part of the line sending up continued, inspiriting shouts. . . . This exuberance continued till the armies arrived at Raleigh. There the news of the President's murder was receiv'd. Then no more shouts or yells, for a week. All the marching was comparatively muffled. . . . A hush and silence pervaded all. (*PW*, I:99–100)

When the troops arrived in Washington in early May, with what Whitman called "the unmistakable Western physiognomy and idioms," he walked with them, and "talk'd with [them] off and on for over an hour," as he helped them to hospital camps. By the end of the month, he had conversed with many—"I am continually meeting and talking with them"—and he admired their "great sociability" and their "largely animal" natures: "I always feel drawn toward the men, and like their personal contact when we are crowded close together, as frequently these days in the street-cars." These soldiers all referred to Sherman as "old Bill" or "uncle Billy," and they talked about the Carolina campaign as they recuperated and readjusted (*PW*, I:104–6). Whitman listened and began piecing together the incidents that would eventually coalesce into the "Ethiopia" poem.

This was the Civil War foundation of the poem, a narrative by a soldier of Sherman, expressing, in highly artificial form, his confusion over the meaning of a black woman saluting the Union troops. Sherman's troops accomplished, through their discipline, what had seemed impossible, but their discipline was continually threatened by the thousands of freed black slaves who insisted on marching with them and whose presence prompted frequent violence and a general disregard of orders. It is fitting, then, that this soldier/narrator should describe his encounter with the black woman in extraordinarily disciplined terms, even as his confusion threatens to pull the poem apart. The steady rhythm of the poem is as inexorable as Sherman's march to the sea and through the Carolinas. The poem can tolerate pauses, questionings, and reconsiderations no more than Sherman could; there is a single-mindedness in the form of the poem and in the historical moment it records. But through this insistent rhythm and rhyme, there are *only* questions and parenthetical pauses, interruptions and lingerings. Something external (the imposed structure) impels the soldier forward, but something internal fights the inexorable push and tries to pause and understand. The meter and rhyme are at once clear and unmotivated. They come from outside the experience, as impersonal as a military command, but the questionings and the pauses come from within, as halting and mysterious as an ancient black woman with an Ethiopian turban on her head. Betsy Erkkila, in an incisive reading of the poem, sees the "highly conventional form" as a device Whitman uses to keep "the black woman safely at a distance" (*Political Poet*, 241). But it is precisely the black woman who initiates the questions, whose fractured and passive syntax slows the pace, whose "turban'd head" keeps causing the soldier to circle around, repeat, linger, instead of moving on.

Reconstruction Poetics

The poem, we need to remind ourselves again, is not a Civil War poem. It is based on Whitman's talks with Sherman's soldiers about the final major campaign of the Civil War, but it was written during Reconstruction, during the congressional debates that put the whole nation in the position of the soldier/narrator, asking of all black Americans exactly what the soldier asks of the old slave woman: who are you? what do you want? what have you seen? what do you think that we have to offer you? Inscrutable, courteous, defiant, proud, maintaining a dual allegiance to the land from which they had been sundered and to the nation in which they had been enslaved but now were about to experience as free citizens, these new Americans rose up and lingered all the day. They would not go away, and they insisted on saluting the same flag to which the white northerner pledged allegiance.

We need to return again to what Whitman was doing during the time he wrote this poem: attending the congressional debates on the aftermath of the Fourteenth Amendment and on the Reconstruction Act and subsequent Reconstruction legislation. Whitman, like much of the nation, was reconstructing the rationale for the Civil War, as well as reconstructing his view of the place of black Americans in the life of the nation. Whitman was also involved in another kind of reconstruction, the reconstruction of *Leaves of Grass*, a book that now had to absorb the Civil War into its program for America's future. In the summer of 1865, he had published *Drum-Taps* (and *Sequel*), his book of Civil War poems, a book he initially conceived as separate from *Leaves of Grass*. But, by 1867, when he published his fourth edition of *Leaves*, he had already decided that his book would not be honest or complete if it did not assimilate the nation's great trauma, and so he literally sewed the books together, binding *Drum-Taps* into the back of the chaotic 1867 Leaves. Whitman's trial of poetic reconstruction had begun.

"Ethiopia" did not enter *Leaves* until 1870, when it appeared in a short-lived cluster called "Bathed in War's Perfume," a late–Reconstruction gathering of poems that focused on the American flag and sought to focus a united country's attention on it as the maternal symbol: "My sacred one, my mother" (*LGC*, 631). This line comes from "Delicate Cluster," an aptly titled poem in this grouping of flag poems, in which the flag must balance its symbols of "teeming life" with its dark meaning as the "Flag of death!" "Delicate Cluster" precedes "Ethiopia" and contains this striking description of the flag: "Ah my silvery beauty! ah my woolly white and crimson! / Ah to sing the song of you, my matron mighty!" The slave woman's "woolly-white and turban'd head" thus unavoidably echoes this line, and her mysterious matronly qualities (qualities that Whitman, as we have seen, always associated with old black women) link her firmly with all that the flag represents. She is literally woven into the textile that is America, her woolly-white head part of the woolly-white of the flag, her greeting of the colors indeed "fateful," since her fate is